REPRINTS OF ECONOMIC CLASSICS

THE TRADE CYCLE

THE TRADE CYCLE

AN ESSAY

BY

R. F. HARROD

STUDENT OF CHRIST CHURCH

REPRINTS OF ECONOMIC CLASSICS

AUGUSTUS M. KELLEY · PUBLISHER
NEW YORK · 1965

ORIGINAL EDITION 1936
REPRINTED 1961 AND 1965
BY ARRANGEMENT WITH
SIR ROY HARROD

LIBRARY OF CONGRESS CATALOGUE CARD NUMBER
65-25859

PRINTED IN THE UNITED STATES OF AMERICA
by SENTRY PRESS, NEW YORK, N. Y. 10019

TO
MY MOTHER

PREFACE

A NEW theory of the Trade Cycle! I offer this, well knowing that whoever ventures to add to the multifarious literature on this subject must incur the reader's extreme displeasure, if he fails to show that he has something of importance to add. This essay only presents the outline of a theory; and properly, because the facts on which it is based may be summed up in a few broad generalizations about which there is common agreement; to construct a more highly elaborated theory would probably involve going further than these warrant.

There are three main sources from which the ideas that are developed in this volume are derived. (i) There is a well-established relation, vouched for by experience and the laws of arithmetic, between the demand for consumable goods and the demand for durable goods, the essence of which is that the absolute amount of the latter depends primarily on the rate of increase of the former. The implications of this for trade cycle theory are here explored. (ii) Mr. Keynes, in his recent volume, *The General Theory of Unemployment, Interest, and Prices*, has developed certain important ideas concerning the relations between the demand for capital goods, the propensity of the community to save, and its general level of activity and income. Full use is made of these. (iii) I have had occasion in the past to work upon the theory of imperfect competition; the object of this branch of economics has been to bring the general theory of value into closer relation with the facts. The doctrines so developed have proved of relevance to the trade cycle problem.

Although the main ideas upon which it is based are drawn from three separate sources, the theory here presented is itself single and indivisible. I should claim on its behalf that a larger number of the special phenomena of the trade cycle are accounted for as the necessary consequences of its central propositions than are accounted for by any other theory.

There is another aspect of this essay to which I wish to draw attention. Much has been heard recently of the desirability of making economic theory more 'dynamic'. A successful attempt to do this should involve the formulation of a new set of propositions, relating to the increase of wealth and income, having the same cogency and demonstrated by the same kind of methods as those of static theory. In fact, writers seeking to introduce dynamic considerations have often tended to confine themselves to mere description or to develop a theory regarding time-lags. But is not a theory of time-lags or of friction premature when the fundamental propositions relating to velocity and acceleration remain unformulated?

The characteristic method of static analysis is to suppose that in certain circumstances a certain set of prices is established. Next it is considered whether individuals, having the tastes and needs that they have in those circumstances, can improve their position by altering their line of conduct. If they cannot, the prices are said to be in equilibrium, and it is assumed that they will remain unchanged until some change in the circumstances occurs. By this method of reasoning a set of most instructive propositions, sometimes known as the laws of supply and demand, has been established. The weak point in the static theory is that, in order not to be too remote from the facts, it is often assumed that one line of action, which individuals take, is to save so and so much. An attempt is made to demonstrate what determines the equilibrium price for this saving, viz. the rate of interest. Yet really the supposition of saving is inconsistent with the pre-requisites of a static analysis, for, if any net saving is occurring, the quantity of capital and the income-earning capacity of the community must be growing, and the factor of growth does not appear among the static assumptions.

An attempt has been made in this essay to adopt a procedure in relation to the factor of growth similar to that of static analysis, to seek, namely, for the moving equilibrium of a steady rate of growth, by asking what sort of action we must suppose individuals to take in certain circumstances, so that, having regard to the circumstances and the factor of growth which their action entails, they will not be able to improve their position otherwise than by continuing to act as they do. The consequences of this attempt are embodied in my theory of the 'dynamic determinants'.

The procedure is, so far as I know, a new one. If it be judged to have had even a partial success in this analysis, the way appears to be open for a great and important extension of economic theory along these lines.

My chief debt of gratitude is to Mr. J. M. Keynes, whose brilliant lucidity, great constructive power, and fine discernment of what factors are likely to be important have done so much to advance understanding in this field. Readers well acquainted with his writings will find traces of his influence at many points in this essay, besides those at which specific reference to him is made.

I am also grateful to Prof. D. H. Macgregor for his encouragement and for a number of valuable suggestions. Mr. J. E. Meade and Mr. W. M. Allen have read through these pages, and their acute comments have enabled me to make various improvements. To Mr. H. D. Henderson I am indebted for giving me a lucid and helpful explanation of his difficulties. The proof sheets have been inspected by the vigilant eye of Mr. R. H. Dundas. To all of these I extend my thanks.

CONTENTS

CHAPTER I

THE HUMAN FACTOR

I. *Preliminary*

THE most fundamental feature of the trade cycle is fluctuation of activity and output. As a preliminary to seeking an explanation of this fluctuation it seems natural to ask the question—what are the circumstances which we should expect to govern the level of activity? Various hypotheses have been put forward with regard to the causes of fluctuation; examination of these cannot be effectively undertaken unless in the first instance our ideas are clear as to the kind of forces that, whether there be fluctuation or not, cause the level of activity to be what it is. Happily we do know broadly why man engages in economic activity. It should be possible to reduce the matter to its simplest terms and then to enumerate the circumstances which appear relevant to the settlement of how much activity he will desire to engage in. With this in view we shall begin by adopting the well-known device of considering the régime of Robinson Crusoe and then introduce successive complications. The value of this procedure may be judged by its results.

For Crusoe the relevant circumstances determining the amount of work he does may be reduced to three, namely, (i) his desire for the various products attainable by work, (ii) his dislike of work, and (iii) the power of his work to achieve the results aimed at. Mention should be made at the outset of one very important circumstance of which it is proposed for convenience to take no account at this stage, namely, that his work is divided between that directed to producing results immediately accessible and that directed to producing results which will occur at a future date. It is assumed for the time being that all the fruits of his endeavour are yielded concurrently with the application of it.

Introspection should make it clear that this list of three governing circumstances is exhaustive. Some economic methodologists have held that introspection should be eschewed in economic analysis. Considered as a piece of abstract reasoning, their case is a good one. But tested by the actual achievements of economics, such as they are, it will not stand. If illicit assumptions implying introspection were weeded out and pseudo-scientific jargon stripped away, the achievements of the general theory of economics would hardly amount to more than nothing at all. The subject is an immature one; progress is more likely to be made if its frailties are recognized; the precocious adoption of methods alleged to be rigorous is apt to lead to the amassing of mere verbiage; verbiage may be expressed in mathematical symbols and remain mere verbiage.

One concession may be made to sceptics about the claim to completeness of the list of three determinants. The claim assumes that Crusoe is alive to what he is doing and acting with deliberation and knowledge. He may indeed become a creature of habit and continue to sow where he can no longer reap. It is assumed in these pages that he acts in his own best interest. This proviso may well be borne in mind as the argument is carried farther and elaborations introduced.

Each of the determinants listed is an omnibus term. Crusoe's 'desire for the various products' consists in fact of his desire for this product and that product. If his desire for one product increases while his desire for each of the others remains the same, we may say that his 'desire for the various products' has increased. But if his desire for one increases while that for another decreases, has his 'desire for the various products' increased or decreased? It is not possible to answer precisely. If one product bulks large in his economy while the other is quite unimportant, the answer may be forthcoming. There is some temptation to put a finer point upon the matter and say that if, his attitude to work and the power of his work to achieve results remaining the same, he works harder as a result of the change, his desire for goods in general must have increased. But the truth of the *ceteris paribus* clause here introduced can only be verified by introspection, and this may be too crude a method to settle the matter if the changes are small. Or, again, an attempt might be made to secure precision by taking the changes of desire one at a time, so that each change was unequivocally either an increase or a decrease. But this would not be satisfactory. If his inclination shifts from oranges to bananas, the decreased desire for oranges clearly cannot be treated as a phenomenon separable from his increased desire for bananas.

It must be observed that the independence of the three determinants could not be maintained without introspection, and even with introspection there may be some blurring. If he works harder at some particular line, is this due to increased desire for the product or decreased disinclination for that particular kind of work? External observation cannot discriminate. If his work in some line becomes more effective, is this due to the increased power of his work or to increased intensity of effort due to decreased disinclination? This cannot be decided by observing how much time he devotes to this line; for his change of inclination might take the form of a decreased disinclination to put muscle into it, unaccompanied by any increased willingness to spend longer at it.

This blurring of the line distinguishing the three determinants from one another is not of great importance. At no point in the subsequent argument will it be desired to distinguish the first very sharply from the second. The distinction between the first two together and the third does come into play, and in this case it seems that even external observation should be able to discriminate with fair precision whether an increase or decrease of output per hour is due to a change of power or of effort.

Under the head of the third determinant, the power of

work to produce results, are subsumed changes in the external environment. Thus better weather for the crops is taken to involve an increase in the power of work. Finding himself able to achieve his desired results more easily, or finding that as a result of given efforts he has greater stocks of desired goods in hand than usual, Crusoe might feel disposed to slack off. If the procession of climatic conditions obeyed a cyclical rhythm, it might be surmised that the level of Crusoe's activity would do so too. Hence the attempt to construct a harvest theory of cycles in trade. Climatic conditions might also influence his inclination to work and his zest for enjoying the fruits of work. Attempts have also been made to connect the trade cycle with climatic cycles affecting the physique. Climatic theories of the cycle are felt to be satisfying because they relate it to the most fundamental features of man's struggle with nature. The multifarious phenomena of banking and finance can then be relegated to their proper place, that of being mere instruments and intermediaries by which the fundamental forces do their predestined work. We are reluctant to suppose that man's course of endeavour can be governed by something so superficial and artificial as his own banking system. Unhappily the climatic theories have not received empirical verification. Climatic changes may prove to play a subordinate part when all is elucidated; it is unlikely that they are of major importance. This result, although disappointing from the point of view already mentioned, is satisfactory in another way. Historical evidence suggests that the amplitude of the cycle has increased in the most recent period; climatic theories would give no reason for this. Indeed, the specifically harvest theories would, if correct, point in the opposite direction: for the importance of man's struggle with nature to obtain raw materials has been steadily dwindling in relation to his total economic activity.

So far we have been considering the relevance of the three determinants in governing Crusoe's action. He has to consider how much he wants the thing, how much work he will have to do in order to get it, and how much he dislikes that work. Let him assess these values and his problem is solved. If from year to year no changes occur in these values, no change may be expected to occur in the level of his activity. Next it is necessary to consider the way in which these forces hold that level of activity in equilibrium.

1. The commodities which he can acquire by work may be arranged in an order of preference. They can also be varied in amount, and, if any amount of one, supposed to accrue to him per annum, is divided into parts, called first, second, third, &c., he prefers the first to the second, the second to the third, &c. This proposition may be related to a physiological law of diminishing reaction to stimuli. It may also be considered by reference to the occasions of use. These occasions may be arranged in an order of preference, e.g. the use of fuel for heating on different days of the year, and since, if he has only one part of fuel he will use it on the preferred, perhaps the coldest, day, whereas if he has two he will use them on the coldest and the next coldest days, he may be said to prefer the first to the second, the second to the third, &c. Thus in regard to all commodities which he can acquire by work and their respective parts, there is an order of preference. This fact is often characterized as the Law of Diminishing Utility of commodities. The utility is here considered as a function of the amount of commodities accruing per unit of time. It is assumed that, if he is in doubt whether to vary his work at any time so as to produce $n+1$ instead of n units of commodities, the $(n+1)$th unit, the extra unit he is considering whether to produce, stands lower on his list of preferences than any of the n units which he intends to produce anyhow. Units may be measured in the following way. Parts of the same commodity constitute equal units if they are physically interchangeable. Parts of different commodities may be

reduced to common units by taking as a unit of B that amount which may be produced with the same amount of work as a unit of A, when he is producing amounts of A and B fairly representative of his normal behaviour.

2. Standing over against this law is the Law of Increasing Dis-utility of work. Dis-utility is considered as a function of the amount of work done per unit period. This law may be related to the increasing fatigue and strain of working more hours per day. Or it may be related to the preference for alternative occupations. Work done to acquire commodities may be agreeable, but it is not the only possible way of spending time. Alternative ways may be placed on a preference list. Work spent on commodities excludes some of these possibilities. It is assumed that to give time for production the lowest items on the list are struck out. If more time is required, a further encroachment on the list of other agreeable occupations must be made.

On the assumption (further considered below) that the power of his work to produce goods is independent of the amount of work he does, it is evident that in virtue of these two laws the level of his activity will be held stable and not change so long as the values of the three determinants enumerated above do not change. The strength of his inclination to obtain extra commodities diminishes as the amount of commodities supposed to accrue to him per unit of time increases. The strength of his disinclination to work for commodities increases in respect of increasing amounts of work undertaken by him per unit of time. It might be that his disinclination to work exceeded his inclination to acquire any commodities at all: his level of activity would then be determined at nil. He gives up hope and abandons the struggle for existence. But if his desire to live is strong enough to make him do some work, the amount he does is fixed at the point at which the inclination to obtain the least-desired (marginal) commodity which he does obtain is neither more nor less than his disinclination to do the last (marginal) particle of work per day that he does. Work harder he will not, for the disinclination exceeds the inclination; nor will he work less hard, for in respect of all the work up to the margin his inclination exceeds his disinclination.

The strength of his inclination and his disinclination have been called 'determinants'. A change in the value of either of these would, unless they happened to cancel each other out exactly, alter his level of activity. The laws of diminishing utility of goods and increasing disutility of effort may be called stabilizing forces or stabilizers. For it is in virtue of these that, the power of his work to produce goods remaining the same, he is indisposed to change his level of activity. The power of these forces to stabilize his level of activity depends on the rate at which the utility decreases and the disutility increases. The sharper the rate of decline of utility and the rate of increase of disutility, the bigger the mistake which any divergence from the prescribed level of activity would involve, and the more speedily would he return to his old position. If, on the other hand, the rates of increase and decrease are small, he may move away from his position without being made sharply aware of his mistake, and the stability of his equilibrium position is *pro tanto* less. If it could happen that in the neighbourhood of the level of work chosen the laws were in suspense, he would be free to vary his level of activity in response to the merest whim, and he could not be said to have a determinate equilibrium level of output at all. But we cannot suppose that these laws are ever actually in suspense, and his equilibrium level is determinate, the degree of stability depending on the severity with which 'stabilizing forces' operate.

3. The third and last remaining determinant of Crusoe's activity is the power of his work to produce commodities. Associated with this will be a third stabilizing force, if the power of his work is governed by what is known as the

Law of Diminishing Returns. This law is in operation if the amount of any commodity which he can obtain for a unit of his work diminishes the more work he does per unit period. It may be due to the niggardliness of nature, to the limited quantity of physical resources on the island, or to the diminishing effectiveness of longer hours of work. If this law is in operation, it is a 'stabilizer'. Not only will Crusoe be held back from further efforts by the decreasing utility of extra supplies and by the increasing disutility of his additional efforts, but also by the fact that the power of his additional efforts to produce commodities decreases.

In Crusoe conditions we may assume that the law is in operation.

It may be noted that owing to the blurring of concepts already mentioned it is not easy to draw a hard and fast line between the law of diminishing returns and the law of increasing disutility of work. If the amount of work done is measured solely by the number of hours devoted to it, the distinction is perfectly plain. But work is sometimes said to have two dimensions, duration and intensity. If intensity is measured by output, then the Law of Diminishing Returns disappears, for a unit increase of work is defined as that amount of work which causes a unit increase of output. If intensity is measured by subjective distaste, then the Law of Increasing Disutility disappears, for a unit increase of work is defined as that amount for which the subjective distaste is no greater than that for the preceding unit. Neither measure is satisfactory; something intermediate is required, since it is expedient to have a measure which makes sense of both laws; demarcation is easier in the more complicated conditions to be explored hereafter.

Next, it is necessary to determine what effect a change in this, the third, determinant will have on the level of activity. About this it is impossible to dogmatize. But some general considerations and observation suggest that an increase of power reduces the amount of work. Part of the benefit of increased power is taken out in additional leisure. As the conditions of man's struggle with nature are relaxed, he relaxes his efforts also. The tendency in the course of progress for the average length of the working day to be reduced is a matter of wide observation.[1] Where the maximum endurable effort is required for bare subsistence, it will be given. But when men are better placed than this, it is known that they voluntarily restrict the amount of their working time. Many goods require leisure for their proper enjoyment. The calendar day is available for the production of goods and their enjoyment. If something can be saved from the time devoted to the production of a given set, only part of the time released is likely to be devoted to producing more, since if some extra leisure can also be acquired by that release, the satisfaction derived from each item of the extra goods will be greater.[2]

To summarize, in Crusoe conditions there are three fundamental conditions, the values of which are relevant to the level of activity chosen. With each of these is associated a stabilizing force. Those associated with the first two are of universal application; the other, the Law of Diminishing Returns, may not always operate. A decrease in the desire for commodities, or an increase in the disinclination to work, diminishes the level of activity, and conversely. An increase in the power of work probably diminishes the level of activity, and conversely.

The terms 'determinant' and 'stabilizer' or 'stabilizing force' have been used and will recur. It is important that their meaning should be defined precisely and clearly understood. A determinant is any consideration relevant to the decision whether to do a given piece of work. The

[1] For the analysis of this within a limited field, see Professor Paul Douglas, *Theory of Wages*, ch. 12.

[2] The contention of this paragraph is equivalent to the proposition that, as income grows, the rate of shrinkage of the utility of extra units is greater than the rate of growth of income.

desire for goods is an example of a determinant. The amount of force with which a determinant acts in inducing a man to work or in deflecting him from work is called its value. Thus if the disinclination to work or the power of work to produce goods changes, the value of that determinant is said to change. But this value is not a simple relation; we speak of the determinants having a given value at any particular time and changing in value from time to time; but at any particular time the pull of the force inducing a man to work is not irrespective of the amount of work he does; if he increases his output the inducement arising from his desire for goods is weaker at the margin. The value of a determinant is thus a complex term; it refers to a whole set of inducements (or deterrents) of differing forces, namely, the inducements which operate at the margin if he produces n units, if he produces $n+1$ units, if he produces $n+2$ units, &c. Suppose we are considering the determinant constituted by his desire for goods; if, owing to some change in one of the *other* determinants, he increases output from n to $(n+2)$ units, the pull of the force constituted by his desire for goods at the margin is less than it was before. But we do not say that the value of the determinant constituted by his desire for goods has altered. That only alters if the pull of his desire for an extra unit of goods when he is producing n units is more or less than it was before when he was producing n units, the pull if he produces $(n+1)$ units is more or less than it was before if he produced $(n+1)$ units, &c. A change in the value of a determinant involves a change in a whole set of these pulls. This is clearly what we mean when we say that our desire for goods or for a certain type of goods has increased. And so with the other determinants.

If for any value of a determinant it is true that the pull of the inducement to work is less or the pull of the force deflecting from work is greater at the margin (i.e. in respect of the last unit of work done), the more work is done per unit of time (e.g. per day or per week), that determinant is called a stabilizer. If for any value of a determinant it is true that the pull of the inducement to work or the pull of the force deflecting from work at the margin is the same, however much work is done per unit of time, that determinant is called neutral. And if for any value of a determinant it is true that the pull of the inducement to work is greater or the pull of the force deflecting from work is less at the margin, the more work is done per unit of time, that determinant is called a de-stabilizer. Thus the determinant constituted by the power of work per unit to produce goods is a stabilizer if the Law of Diminishing Returns is in operation. But if the converse Law, that of Increasing Returns, were in operation, that determinant would be a de-stabilizer. And if the power of work was independent of the amount put in per day, that determinant would be neutral.

An approach to the conditions of the real world is conducted in three stages in this chapter. Complications connected with the division of work into work for concurrently available goods and work for future goods are postponed to the next chapter.

The stages considered in this chapter may be set out as follows:

1. The division of labour.
2. The capitalist system (excluding that feature mentioned in the foregoing paragraph).
3. The monetary system.

Not all aspects of these complications are considered: attention is confined to the question of how far they affect the three determinants and three stabilizing forces either by adding new ones or eliminating those which exist in the Crusoe state.

II. *The Division of Labour*

The division of labour has two aspects, co-operation and specialization. Problems arising under the former head are considered in the second section (capitalist system). Here we shall assume that there are a multiplicity of producers, of whom each specializes in the production of a single product which he exchanges for the objects of his desire.

It is clear from the outset that a fourth determinant has already appeared on the scene, namely, the rate at which the individual producer can exchange his product for the objects of his desire. This is additional to the other three. A change in the rate at which the producer can exchange his product for other things is clearly relevant to the amount of work he does. It will have the same kind of effect on his activity as a change in the power of his work. He will bless Providence equally whether he becomes able to produce more goods with the same amount of effort and so, at the old rate of exchange, to acquire more of the objects of his desire for a given amount of effort, or, the effectiveness of his efforts remaining the same, the rate of exchange moves in his favour and he can acquire more objects of desire for a given amount of effort in that way.

If, as we argued above, his level of activity is likely to vary inversely with its effectiveness, it is also likely to fall if the rate of exchange becomes more favourable and to rise if it becomes less favourable.

Is there a fourth stabilizing force associated with this fourth determinant? In order to answer this question it is necessary to draw a distinction between conditions of 'perfect competition' and those of 'imperfect competition' (including monopoly). In conditions of perfect competition, we suppose a great number of producers engaged on making the same homogeneous interchangeable stuff which can be exchanged in an organized market. In this case variations in the amount which an individual chooses to produce do not appreciably affect the total amount to be disposed of in the market, and so do not affect the rate at which it is exchanged for other goods in the market. In this case no new stabilizing force is associated with the fourth determinant. Suppose the individual mistakenly to produce too much, namely, more than his equilibrium output. His mistake will be made apparent by the cumulative effect of three forces. The extra commodities he acquires have less utility per unit than the marginal unit acquired when he was in the equilibrium position; the extra work he does has greater disutility per unit than the marginal work of equilibrium; and the extra work yields per unit less units of produce than he was obtaining for his marginal effort in equilibrium. The more rapidly the utility of goods diminishes for him and the disutility of his work increases and the physical returns to his work diminish, the harder the rap on the knuckles which the 'laws of nature' will administer to him for his mistake. The rap obtains no further force from the law of exchange. For he will still be able to exchange his extra output for the goods he desires at the same rate of exchange per unit as before.

In conditions of imperfect competition the case is otherwise, and with the fourth determinant is associated a fourth stabilizing force. If the market is narrow, if the number of producers of the particular article is small, if the article is not homogeneous, if the market is not organized, or if buyers are attached by ties of habit, custom, or business friendship to particular producers, the individual producer will have to take less per unit in exchange for his extra output. And he will be proved wrong for having advanced beyond his equilibrium position for a fourth reason. It may be observed that conditions of imperfect competition apply to almost all producers, other than those of primary products, in the modern world.

So far so good. But when we pass from the Crusoe state to a society with a number of individual, specialist producers living by exchange of goods, a new problem appears on the horizon, namely, that of the equilibrium level of output of the community as a whole. In considering the equilibrium of the individual the rate at which he could exchange his produce was taken as a given datum external to himself. In imperfect competition this rate might indeed be altered by his own action, but the range of rates which he could get in response to various possible levels of his own output could not. But as well as considering the equilibrium of the individual it is necessary to consider that of the whole community.

First, we may set aside a preliminary difficulty. For the community as a whole to be in equilibrium every individual in it must be so, in accordance with the four determinants. But it may happen that an individual in employment A, having adjusted his level of activity to the best of his ability, still feels he is worse off than he would be in employment B. At this stage it is expedient to assume complete mobility between employments, so that the individual finding himself in this position is able to transfer himself and does transfer himself to employment B. Thus, in full equilibrium not only will every one have adjusted his output properly within his employment, but will have chosen his employment, so that no one can gain anything by a further change of occupation.

This being so, if any individual oversteps the mark he will be punished in three (or four) ways. What will happen if the whole community jointly oversteps the mark? The three primary stabilizers being in operation, each individual will tend, so far as these are concerned, to be as severely punished by joint as by individual excess. Co-operation in error will not exempt individuals from the effects of the laws of diminishing utility, increasing disutility, or diminishing returns. The incidence of the punishment may, however, be different in the case of a conjoint advance, as this may alter the rates of exchange favourably to some, unfavourably to other, individuals. In order to get rid of these differences and to isolate a further problem for consideration, let us suppose a joint and uniform advance, uniform advance being defined as the condition in which each increases output by so much that the rates of exchange between commodities are not altered. A uniform increase of output by all will thus not be the same as an equi-proportional increase by all. For as more goods come on to the market, desires for equi-proportional increments of each may not be proportional in intensity to the marginal desires for the amounts formerly produced (demands for various commodities may not have equal 'elasticities'). Thus equi-proportional increases of all commodities might not leave their relative market values unchanged. But there must be *some* set of ratios between the increments of various commodities which would leave their relative values (rates of exchange against one another) unchanged. And an increase of all commodities with the increments standing in these ratios we define as a uniform increase.[1]

If every member of the community were working in conditions of perfect competition, the equilibrium of the output of the whole community would be maintained by the three stabilizers only, and no fourth is to be added thereto. For since a uniform advance would leave price ratios unchanged, no individual would be damnified, so far as his price ratio was concerned, by a uniform advance. Every individual would be damnified by the operation of the three primary laws. That is all. There is no fourth law, no 'law of exchange', which could injure him in the event of a joint and uniform departure from a given position of equilibrium.

But how stands the matter when conditions of imperfect competition are widely prevalent? The elucidation of this is a little more complicated than anything that has gone before. The reader's attention is craved, since the solution of this problem will prove of interest in later sections of our story.

An individual undertaking an isolated increase of output in conditions of imperfect competition has to face a move-

[1] In certain exceptional cases the output of *some* commodities might have to be decreased in order to fulfil the condition for a uniform advance.

ment of the rate of exchange against him. But if the increase is joint and uniform, no alteration in the rates of exchange occurs. Does this mean that if the expansion is joint and uniform, the fourth determinant exerts no stabilizing force upon the output of the community as a whole? If this is so, it is clearly an important conclusion. When we have explored and exposed the further complications of a fully modern economy, we shall find that the three primary stabilizers lose much of their pristine force. It will be of interest to know whether the fourth determinant is likely to produce a stabilizing effect.

The matter is not settled by showing that with a uniform advance value ratios remain the same. It is necessary to examine more closely the economics of imperfect competition. The notion of 'marginal revenue' here is central. In these conditions the rate at which the individual producer can sell his goods depends on the amount he produces. If he expands output from n to $(n+1)$ units per day, the amount of other goods he gets per unit of his own is less than when he was only trying to dispose of n per day. But the extra amount of goods he gets in exchange for his increment of output is not measured by the amount he gets for one unit at the rate at which he can sell when he disposes of $(n+1)$; it is that amount less what he loses by reason of the fact that he has to dispose of all n units at a lower rate.[1] Put otherwise it is the receipts accruing if he disposes of $(n+1)$ units less the receipts accruing if he disposes of n units. This remainder, which is the actual gain in goods due to his increasing output from n to $(n+1)$ units, is known as marginal revenue.

[1] He may not make this loss if he is able to discriminate among his customers, charging them different prices. But in this case it is necessary to take the average price he gets in order to determine what a uniform advance is in accordance with the definition. In these circumstances marginal revenue will stand in the same relation to the average price received, as marginal revenue stands to *the* price in the conditions envisaged in the text; the further argument of the text covers the case of price discrimination *mutatis mutandis*—average price being written for *the* price.

Now the fact that price ratios after a uniform expansion are the same as before does not guarantee that marginal revenues to all producers are the same. If marginal revenues fall all round as a result of the uniform increase, then each and every producer will suffer disappointment, and there will be a force arising from this source driving them back to their old equilibrium, in fact a fourth stabilizer.

It must be understood that, after the uniform advance has occurred, the marginal revenue accruing to each producer will not be equal to the difference between the receipts of each when all produced n units and the receipts of each when, all having made a uniform advance, each produces $(n+1)$.[1] Since the definition of a uniform advance is that exchange ratios remain the same, the difference referred to in the last sentence is the same as the price of one unit when $(n+1)$ are produced. The marginal revenue for each producer, on the other hand, is the difference between his receipts when he and all produce $(n+1)$ and his receipts when he produces n and the others continue to produce $(n+1)$. To be in equilibrium the individual must feel that he is doing right for himself, given that the others do what they do. Therefore the marginal revenue to him in the new position, by which he has to judge whether to stay in the $(n+1)$ position or to recede back to the n position, is the difference between what he gets at $(n+1)$ and what he gets at n, supposing that the others will stay put at $(n+1)$ in either case. Now this difference depends on the degree of unwillingness of his buyers to substitute other goods for his at the margin; and there is no reason why this should be the same after the uniform advance as before it, although relative prices are the same. In the new state there are more goods and every one is richer; their attitude to potential shifts in their expenditure in response to possible price changes

[1] In this sentence the unit of output must be taken to be defined conformably with the definition of uniform advance given above.

may be quite different—their 'elasticities of demand' for each and every commodity may be different. What does this mean for the individual producer? When all the world was poor (each producing n units only) the loss per unit which the individual would have to incur if he increased sales from n to $(n+1)$ might have been 1d. per unit.[1] In the general advance he was able to push on from n to $(n+1)$ without losing anything per unit (price ratios remained the same). But now, when all the world is rich, it may happen that if he retraced his steps he could put up his price by 2d. per unit and only lose one unit of sales, i.e. retreat from $(n+1)$ to n. To make the matter still more concrete let us name a price for his wares, say 10s. per unit. In the old state of affairs in a poor world his marginal revenue at an output of n units was 10s.$-(n \times 1d.)$, 10s. being the price per unit when he produces n units and 1d. being the variation in the price per unit resulting from his varying his output by one unit. In the new state of affairs he can sell $(n+1)$ units at 10s., demand being higher because every one is richer. But his marginal revenue at an output of $(n+1)$ is only 10s.$-(n \times 2d.)$. In this case, the world having become richer is less willing to vary its consumption of his goods in response to a given price-change, i.e. needs a bigger price-change to induce it to vary consumption by a given amount. In these circumstances, although the price after the uniform advance remains the same (10s.), marginal revenue has fallen. If this is a representative plight for the individual, each one will feel that he has done wrong, and the fourth stabilizer will be in operation.

Is it a representative plight? In the event of a uniform advance what may be expected to happen to the average of marginal revenues? It may be the same or different, it may be greater or less on balance. This being so, it would seem that we must conclude that in conditions

---

[1] 1d. and other money figures in this context must be taken to represent the power of purchasing a given quantity of the goods he desires.

of imperfect competition it is impossible to state *a priori* whether the fourth stabilizer will be operating upon the level of output in the community as a whole or not. If marginal revenues are in general lower, it will be in operation, but if they are in general higher, there will in fact be a de-stabilizing force associated with the fourth determinant. If after the uniform advance marginal revenues are on balance higher, individuals will be better off so far as exchange receipts due to the marginal output are concerned, and this might offset the worsening of their position due to the operation of the three primary stabilizers. If this actually happened, the system as a whole would be in neutral equilibrium as between the former and later level of output. And it might even be in neutral equilibrium over a wide range. The probability, however, of this exact balance of opposing forces (stabilizing and de-stabilizing) is remote.

So far we appear to be in ignorance with regard to the stabilizing or de-stabilizing effect of the fourth determinant upon the output of the community as a whole. I propose to argue, however, for its having a stabilizing effect. Up to now every proposition advanced, possibly with one exception,[1] may be taken to be as certain as anything in economic theory. In the following section we enter into the realm of conjecture and opinion. Let the reader take warning.

As a result of the uniform advance contemplated, every one produces more and every one is richer in goods. Every one is able to consume goods lower on his scale of preference. This has been expressed in the proposition that the marginal utility of a penny to every one is lower. Now there does seem reason to suppose that in this state of affairs every one will be less sensitive to price differences. They will be more inclined, like the rich man, to have what they want and let the expense be damned.

[1] The inverse relation between the power of work and the amount of activity.

If put in a crude form this argument might rightly be counted fallacious. Suppose that a commodity rises in price by 1*d*. That penny means less to the richer community, and the price-rise might be thought to be less of a deterrent to purchase. So stated the point is wrong. For if the penny has less utility to the richer community, so also has the marginal unit of any particular commodity purchased. The ratio of the utility of the penny to the utility of the marginal unit of the commodity may in general be expected to be the same, and the same also therefore the deterrent effect on purchase of the rise of price by a penny. The point requires more subtle statement.

In the ordinary course of affairs people have their desires, habits, and inclinations, but they have to think of the cost. Their incomes are limited, and on frequent occasions they have to think of the price of enjoyment. There may often be a line of least resistance in expenditure which is not always the path of the greatest enjoyment. They should and must pause from time to time to think, 'Is this the wisest plan?' That bother about the cost is something which may legitimately be abstracted from the general balance of their pleasures and pains and considered as a disutility in and by itself. A man may often find it more satisfactory to take the line of least resistance, a line of habit it may be, even though the total sum of enjoyment *in the absence of the actual bother about readjustment* would be greater as a result of some readjustment. In other words, he may waste money on some wonted pursuits, money which, if saved, would bring him in a substantial balance of pleasure; yet that balance of pleasure may be less than the inconvenience of changing his wonted pursuits. Some like to think of money on as few particular occasions as possible, because it reminds them of the general limitations of the human lot and their own disappointments and frustrations; better to waste a little than to recur to that irritating theme. But more practical difficulties are involved—and these apply to purchases

within the business world itself; it may take much time
and trouble to find the 'cheapest market'. Now although
the utility of the extra penny on the price may bear the
same ratio to the marginal utility of the commodity in a
state of affluence as in one of impoverishment, it may bear
a very different ratio to the trouble of readjustment. The
utility of the extra penny is undoubtedly lower, but there
is no reason to suppose that the trouble of readjustment
will be. As the utility of commodities consumed on the
margin declines, as the pressure exerted by a shortage of
funds on all purchases is relaxed, the troubles of adjustment loom larger. It becomes more sensible to follow
the line of least resistance at the cost of wastage, since the
marginal pleasures foregone in consequence of it are of
less absolute importance and therefore more likely to be
inadequate to compensate for the trouble of avoiding waste.

It might be thought that these matters are pettifogging
and of too little importance for inclusion in our survey at
its present stage of broad outline. But it is now agreed
that imperfections in competition are matters of first-rate
importance, and that devotion to habit and the line of
least resistance are leading causes of imperfection. Moreover, we are considering the operation of the fourth determinant in a world in which imperfect competition is
assumed to be prevalent; we are justified then in considering how imperfect competition reacts on the fourth
determinant through purchasers' behaviour. The burden
of this argument is that imperfections may be expected to
increase as the community gets more affluent. If this is
right, it may in part account for the increasing attention
paid by students to imperfect competition in modern
conditions.

If the generalization of the foregoing paragraphs is
accepted, it might properly be named the Law of Diminishing Elasticity of Demand, which means that, as output as a whole increases and individuals become more
affluent, their sensitiveness to price differences declines.

It would constitute a fourth stabilizer operating upon the level of output as a whole.

One piece of broad evidence may be cited in favour of its operation at this stage, although it involves using concepts which will only be explained subsequently. In a slump, in which we are faced with the converse process, namely, one of increasing impoverishment, it is generally believed that the prices of goods produced in conditions of imperfect competition fall more than their 'marginal costs of production' (*vide infra*). It will be shown that this can only happen either if sellers are just being silly and charging lower prices than are in their interest or, what is more likely, if elasticities of demand have in general increased. But that they should increase is precisely what our theory demands. The matter is one which calls for empirical investigation. It will remain of importance throughout this narrative, although the assumption that the Law does prevail will not be used to establish any of the positive conclusions.

The conclusion reached in this section is that the introduction of division of labour and an exchange economy provides a fourth determinant of the individual's level of activity. With this no fourth stabilizing force will be associated, if conditions of perfect competition prevail. For the individual working in conditions of imperfect competition a fourth stabilizing force is introduced, since when he tries to market additional quantities of his commodity he will have to accept a lower rate of exchange for it. Whether the exchange system provides an additional stabilizer for the output of the community as a whole, when conditions of imperfect competition prevail, is a matter of legitimate doubt. It is argued above that there are grounds for supposing that with imperfect competition is associated a Law of Diminishing Elasticity of Demand. If this is correct, then in conditions of imperfect competition the exchange system provides a fourth stabilizer of the level of activity in the community as a whole.

III. *Capitalism*

In this section one feature of capitalism will be singled out as relevant to the argument at this stage. Further, one aspect of the division of labour, namely, co-operation, was left over for consideration here. Crusoe has complete freedom in the disposal of his time; he can draw the line between work and leisure where he likes. If co-operation in production is necessary or advantageous, this freedom has to be modified in some measure, since the co-operating workers have to dovetail their efforts into one another's, according to some plan. It would be interesting to consider what results this fact entails in a non-capitalist economy; it does not appear, however, to be necessary for our argument to do so. For once we reach the condition of capitalism the co-operation is planned on certain clearly defined principles, and we may proceed direct to the consideration of these.

The use of capital involves the distinction between work expended on concurrently disposable goods and work expended on goods available in future time. But it is not to this cardinal feature of capitalism that it is proposed to draw attention here; on the contrary it is neglected. When we come to that feature we shall be in the very heart of the problem of the trade cycle; and it is the function of this chapter merely to clear the ground by reducing to their simplest terms other elements that govern the level of output.

None the less it is necessary to mention that in a capitalist régime almost all work is carried out in conjunction with more or less durable aids to production embodied in specific forms. These aids were constructed in the past with a view to their prospective yield. The present owner, whether he himself was directly or indirectly responsible for the construction or merely purchased them from a previous owner, incurred the necessary cost or paid the necessary price with a view to their yield. It may be presumed that he will try to secure that this is as great as possible. To do this he will secure the services of those required to collaborate with the fixed aids in order to effect production.

It is necessary to define capitalism more precisely. From one point of view any system of production may be regarded as capitalistic in which the more or less durable aids to production, themselves man-made in the past, play a part of substantial importance in the process. From this point of view the question of who owns the aids is a minor matter. An independent farmer doing his own work mostly, but using very elaborate machinery of all kinds, would be regarded as producing in as fully a capitalist way as a farmer who employed the labour of others to utilize the machinery. There might be a difference in the scale of their operations. But, it would be argued, so far as the capitalist character of the productive process is concerned, one type is as good an instance of capitalism as another. It is the use of much durable equipment, involving as that does a 'roundabout' process of production and 'waiting'—for the efforts originally expended on the production of the durable aids only yield their desired results over a period of time—that is the essence of capitalist production, and the location of the ownership of the durable aids is a merely incidental circumstance of no fundamental importance.

Socialist writers have been inclined to place the emphasis differently. To them the distinction of person between the owner of the means of production and the worker upon them has seemed fundamental. Thus they tend to take a narrower view of the nature of capitalism, and to define it as the system in which the ownership of means of production is divorced from the function of actually using them. For our present purpose it is necessary to adopt this narrower view. It may be noted that in the broader sense almost all production is now capitalistic; but in the narrower sense there are still large spheres, for instance, in agricultural production, in which production is not capitalistic. Independent farmers often own their own tools and land and apply their own labour to them.

The reason why we require the narrower definition is that the location of ownership vitally affects the status of the first two stabilizers. If the tools are owned by the man who works with them, these two retain their pristine force. He acquired the tools in the past in order to increase the effectiveness of his efforts; the excess of the produce of his efforts employed in conjunction with them over the produce which his unaided efforts would yield may be regarded as the specific yield of the tools. No doubt he compared this with the price or cost of them when he acquired them. Having acquired them, the extent to which he employs them, that is, the amount of work he does with their aid, is governed by the four determinants. He will not make any special endeavour, unless he be an eccentric, to make them yield as much as possible. If he finds that when working at a certain rate, the marginal disutility of work exceeds the marginal utility of his produce, he will be inclined to slack off; he will not be deflected therefrom by the thought that harder work would make the tools yield more. The existence of the tools will no doubt cause him to do a different amount of work from what he would do without them; they have an effect on the level of his activity analogous to that produced by any other change in his environment that increases the power of his work. His environment being what it is, the four determinants still govern his level of activity; there is no rival determinant such as, I must make these tools produce their maximum possible physical yield, or—in imperfect competition—I must make these tools produce that yield which when exchanged brings in the maximum possible quantity of goods I desire. It is true that he will endeavour to secure the maximum possible utility from the machines. But that will be achieved precisely by working with their aid up to the margin at which the utility of his product is not greater than the disutility of further effort. The appearance of the tools on the scene still leaves the primary determinants in unchallenged control and the primary stabilizers in effective operation.

The position is truly and substantially different when the owner of the tools does not work them himself but hires other factors to do so. His purpose is to maximize the value of their yield; by so doing he automatically maximizes the net utility accruing to himself from them. The value of their yield consists of the goods which he can get in exchange for their produce less what he has to pay to the factors of production hired to work them. (What he pays them *in* is a matter left over for the next section.) To fulfil his purpose he must arrange production on such a scale that the marginal revenue derived from it is equal to marginal cost. Marginal revenue has already been defined. Marginal cost is the amount he has to pay out in hiring factors of production when he produces n units per week, less what he has to pay out for that purpose when he produces $(n-1)$ units per week. Net revenue is maximized when these two are equated, for if marginal cost exceeded marginal revenue there would be clear loss in respect of part of the output, and if marginal revenue exceeded marginal cost there would be net gain at the margin, and it would clearly be in his interest to push the margin outward, that is, to increase his rate of output and so make more of this net gain until the point was reached when no further net gain could be secured by a further increase. The unskilled reader might for a moment suppose that this process of extending output until net gain at the margin was eliminated would involve the elimination of profit and therefore must be wrong. But that is not so. The elimination of net gain at the margin does not eliminate but maximizes profit. It makes the total revenue from the machines exceed the total cost of hiring labour by the greatest possible amount. The reader may convince himself of this by reflecting on the definitions of marginal cost and marginal revenue. The principle is analogous to that by which Crusoe does so much work that marginal utility is equal to marginal disutility; so long as the utility of what he gets by work exceeds its irksomeness he should go on, but as soon as the irksomeness is felt fully to offset the advantages reaped he should stop. Only so can he make the time at his disposal yield the greatest possible net advantage.

It now appears that the principles governing the amount of work which the owner of the machines gets done in collaboration with them are different from those governing the amount of work independent workers do. And this is important, since the level of activity in a modern community is mainly determined by the amount of work which owners of machines or other forms of fixed capital choose to get done in conjunction with them. The first two determinants disappear from view and their place is taken by a new determinant, namely, the terms on which owners of fixed capital can get the other factors of production to collaborate with them.

Now it may at once be felt that this change is one of form rather than substance, since the collaborating factors are after all none other than the old independent workers in disguise. Will not they be governed in the terms they ask of their employers by those same forces of the utility of goods received as income and the disutility of work? They are still men with the same likes and dislikes. Cannot they make the terms on which they offer their services to employers reflect precisely those likes and dislikes, so that the employers are led to employ them up to the same point at which they would voluntarily choose to work if independent? Unhappily the matter is not quite so simple.

One great difference in the new situation is that when an employer wishes to vary the rate at which his machines are worked, he does not most commonly get an existing labour force to work for longer or shorter hours or with greater or less intensity, but takes on or turns off hands.

The variation much more often takes the form of a change in the number employed than in the amount of work which a given number of employees do. Now if an increase of employment takes the form not of n men working harder but of $n+1$ men being employed and each working as hard as each of the n employed worked before, it is not clear that the increment of work involves a greater balance of disutility to utility than was involved by the work previously done at the margin. This suggests at once that the pristine stabilizers may lose some of their force in the new arrangement.

In the new situation the capitalist owner controls the level of activity. The determinant which now takes the place of the two primary determinants affecting independent workers (utility of goods acquired and disutility of effort) consists of the terms on which the capitalist can hire factors of production. We have now to ask—does this determinant carry with it a stabilizing force? And, if so, is this force as great as that which the two primary stabilizers exerted in non-capitalist conditions?

To answer this question, we may ask another—how ought the terms on which the collaborating factors are willing to supply their services to be regulated if they are to exert the same degree of stabilizing influence on the volume of capitalist activity that the two primary determinants exert on the activity of independent producers? Suppose a capitalist contemplates decreasing activity by one-eighth; and suppose that he is disposed to employ the non-capitalist method of reducing all hours from eight to seven per day. If he paid the same hourly rate each worker would feel that at the margin the utility of his income per penny was greater than before and that the disutility of work per minute was less. He would wish to push back again to the old position. But he cannot do so, for the capitalist employer determines what is to be done. If the gap which now appears between the utility of income and the disutility of work is to be felt by the capitalist as a force leading him to re-expand, it is necessary for that feeling on the part of the worker to be transmitted through to the capitalist by the terms on which he can hire labour becoming more favourable. If that happens, then, *ceteris paribus*, he will tend to return to the old equilibrium. To exert a stabilizing force equal to that of the two primitive stabilizers, the terms on which the collaborating factors offer services should fall in a recession at a rate equal to that at which marginal utility of income increases multiplied by that at which the marginal disutility of labour decreases.

In fact the employer does not in the main pursue this method of curtailing activity, but turns off hands. To cover this situation all we can say is that as unemployment increases, rates of pay should fall at the rate at which they would have to fall by the foregoing formula if the decreased activity took the form entirely of a shorter working day.

In the real world this does not happen. What is left of the two primary stabilizers may be summarized under three heads. (1) Higher rates for overtime. These may provide a notable restraining influence when fixed capital is being worked at full capacity, but are clearly unimportant in relation to fluctuations between points below that of full capacity. (2) When there is a reserve of unemployed, the employer may have some freedom to pick and choose among those available. If in a recession he is able to weed out the weaker brethren the real cost to him of the hired factors per man declines.[1] (3) If unemployment increases there may be a tendency for rates of pay generally to fall. These three facts may be collectively designated by the expression Plasticity of Prime Costs.[2] The stabilizing influence of this plasticity is probably very much less than that of the two primary stabilizers.

[1] In the later chapters, however, this feature (2) is for convenience subsumed under another stabilizer, the Law of Diminishing Returns, viz. as diminishing returns to human material, cf. p. 81.

[2] The technical word 'prime' is here used for the factors which collaborate with the pre-existing aids to production.

It may be well to summarize the results so far achieved. There are three determinants of the capitalist producer's level of output, namely, (i) the rate at which he can hire factors, (ii) the power of those factors to produce, and (iii) the rate at which he can exchange their produce. The stabilizing forces associated with each of these are (i) Plasticity of Prime Costs, (ii) the Law of Diminishing Returns, and (iii)—in imperfect competition only—the Law of Demand. The Law of Demand is the name for the fact that, if in imperfect competition an individual producer expands output, he can only dispose of increments at increasingly unfavourable rates of exchange.

Considering the level of output as a whole in a capitalist community, we confine ourselves to uniform movements of advance and recession. The two stabilizing forces remain as above, but for the law of demand, which does not apply to the community as a whole, we must write the Law of Diminishing Elasticity of Demand. This can only apply if conditions of imperfect competition are predominant, and even then its existence is not certain. These three capitalist determinants and these three capitalist stabilizers and not those of the Crusoe Economy will in future be called *the* three determinants and *the* three stabilizers.

It is time to recur to the Law of Diminishing Returns, which has been neglected in recent pages. Crusoe was confronted with the fact that, with limited natural resources at his disposal, the physical yield to increasing quantities of effort expended by him per unit of time might decline. In the modern world this Law becomes less prominent. An increasing proportion of man's activity is devoted not to the extraction of raw materials from the earth, but to working them up into more and more elaborately finished articles. But to this work of processing or finishing, already the major part and an ever-growing part of the whole of human activity, the Law does not in general apply. Its sphere is curtailed and its influence upon the economic system as a whole is correspondingly diminished. Under capitalism, however, it reappears in a new form. When considering possible variations in output in a very short period the quantity of durable aids to production embodied in various specific forms is taken to be fixed and given, or, anyhow, not capable of easy expansion. In each industry and firm expansion of output is limited by this fact. When plant is worked up to capacity, increased application of the prime factors may meet with very sharply diminishing returns. In a condition of active trade this is undoubtedly an important consideration. But when we consider variations of output below a certain fairly high level, it is doubtful if the law of diminishing returns plays much part. Production in a factory can usually be increased up to the point of capacity without the amount produced by the marginal units of the prime factors falling at all; indeed it may increase; and if it does, in place of this old primary stabilizer we have a de-stabilizing force.

It is now fairly clear that stability in our modern society has become somewhat precarious. The robust and healthy forces which guided the life of Crusoe now appear in an enfeebled and attenuated form. We have (i) the Plasticity of Prime Costs. It is notorious that little reliance can be placed upon this. We have (ii) the Law of Diminishing Returns. In a great part of industry this probably does not operate at all, save in a condition of high activity. It may even be that an inverse law operates in many cases. We have (iii) the Law of Diminishing Elasticity of Demand. The very existence of this is not certainly established. None the less I venture to believe that it is the most important of the three.

If the stabilizing forces were entirely eliminated the level of activity would be quite free to move up or down, provided that the movement were 'uniform'. In the actual course of the trade cycle the movement is not found to be uniform. This is largely connected with the relation between capital and consumable goods, a matter reserved for discussion at a later stage. The lack of uniformity may be connected with the fact that the stabilizing principles or their inverse laws operate with different force in different occupations.

But there is one striking lack of uniformity upon which it is possible to say something as a result of the rudimentary analysis already undertaken, namely, the behaviour of agricultural output and prices in the most recent depressions. Output has been obstinately maintained and prices have fallen out of all proportion. The reasons for this are generally well appreciated, yet not always perfectly appreciated. For mixed with the proper explanation there is generally some alloy of confusion, some notion that the farmers are unduly slow to react, even stupid or obstinate, lacking in the prevision vouchsafed to others, obedient rather to habit than to self-interest. But in fact the observed agricultural phenomena follow quite naturally, nay inevitably, from the analysis already adduced, and the assumption that the farmers have acted in any way injudiciously from their own point of view is unnecessary and unwarranted.

In a general recession the capitalist producer is confronted with a worsening of the terms on which he can dispose of his output. As the output of others declines, their demand for his in terms of goods declines too. Obeying the principle that marginal cost must be equated to marginal revenue, he restricts activity; by so doing he may reduce marginal cost—and on this, if he is in perfect competition, he must rely—but more commonly the chief consequence of restriction is to raise marginal revenue above the value it would have if he continued to attempt to dispose of his former quantity of output to an impoverished world. He meets the fall of demand by restricting the quantity of goods he attempts to sell; he restricts as far as is necessary to maintain marginal revenue at an equality with marginal cost.

But the non-capitalist producer reacts in a different

way. He sees the reduction of demand as a reduction in the power of his labour to acquire the goods he wants by exchange. It is analogous to a weakening of his own power to produce. Our analysis does not show that this is likely to lead to a restriction of activity. On the contrary, if the hypothesis that there is an inverse relation between the power of work and the level of work is correct, he will increase. Now a great part of agricultural production is non-capitalist. (Capitalist is, of course, here used in its narrower sense (*vide supra*).) Consequently we should expect agricultural output to be maintained in a depression. It is erroneous and absurd to argue that when non-capitalist farmers maintain output in a depression, they are being stupid or slow-witted. It is the proper thing for them to do.

The reader may feel some uneasiness on the ground that this argument seems to go too far. If a fall in demand is not met by a reduction of output in the world of independent producers, how comes it that supply is ever adjusted to demand? The answer is twofold. (i) If there is a relative fall for a particular agricultural product, farmers may be able to switch over from this to others, provided that their circumstances do not necessitate specialization on a particular crop. Only where circumstances do require such specialization, e.g. in rubber, coffee, wheat in Saskatchewan, &c., may we expect to find much overproduction of a particular agricultural commodity compared with that of others. (ii) If the decline in demand covers all agricultural products, the farmer has not this way out of his difficulty. None the less supply may be adjusted to demand in the long run, for if his sad plight persists he may cease to be a farmer and find another occupation. Mobility between employments was assumed earlier in this chapter, and, if there was complete mobility in the short period, agricultural output would be restricted in a slump through the rapid exodus of farmers. But it must be remembered that in a slump there is likely to be unemployment in other occupations owing to capitalists turning off hands; and an independent farmer with little liquid capital may well prefer to continue in a poor way rather than join the ranks of the unemployed. The purpose of this paragraph is to indicate that the foregoing arguments do not lead to the absurd conclusion that agricultural output will never be restricted owing to a fall in demand; it merely leads to the conclusion that it is unlikely to be considerably restricted in a slump.

These considerations serve also to elucidate what is in the back of the minds of those who believe that the excessive depression in agriculture is somehow connected with a time-lag. A depression in a trade dominated by independent producers is only likely to be alleviated after a time-lag, especially if the depression occurs during a general slump, since it can only be relieved by these transferring their occupation. Ultimately the same is true in any trade. But in the capitalistic branches producers go half-way to meet the fall in demand by restriction. The time-lag between the onset of a depression and the reduction of output is greater in agriculture than in manufacture. But this is not because the reaction time of agriculturists is greater; it is not because they take longer to appreciate a given situation; if reduction in manufacture only occurred as and when manufacturers withdrew from business, the time-lag would then probably be equally great in that field. Among independent producers the natural and proper reaction to a fall in demand is *not* to reduce output; in their case, unlike that of capitalists, the reduction will and should only occur when the adverse force is a sufficiently long-period one to drive them to seek new fields of enterprise.[1]

[1] It should be noticed that the foregoing argument of the text relates to the distinction between capitalist and non-capitalist producers, and *not* to that between perfectly competitive producers and those working for an imperfect market. The second distinction is no doubt also of interest in this connexion. In certain conditions governing their cost schedules, perfectly competitive capitalists may react to a recession in the same way

The observed reaction of agriculturists in recent depressions brings out in a striking way the importance of that feature of capitalism which we have been considering in this section for trade cycle study. If all producers reacted like the agriculturists to a fall in demand, there would be no substantial restriction of output—and therefore no substantial fall in demand. In fact the trade cycle would not occur, or, we should rather say, if it occurred, it would take quite a different form from that with which we are familiar. Fundamentally, those who advocate greater plasticity of prime costs as a recipe for alleviating the cycle wish to make manufacturers behave as agriculturists do in fact behave. There is another school of thought which desires to see the agriculturists behave like the manufacturers and form restrictive agreements. They argue that if the total income accruing to them were maintained, their demand for other goods would not fall off so much, and the level of activity in the whole field would be better sustained. Such an argument is not related to the analysis of this chapter and indeed does not appear to be grounded on fundamental theory; I have the impression that it is *ad hoc* and superficial. Both these recipes must be put into cold storage at present and consideration of their merits postponed until a later stage.

IV. *The Monetary System*

The foregoing argument, as it crept forward step by step, referred to producers first making goods for their enjoyment, then exchanging them for others, and finally paying other factors of production, the prime factors, for their collaboration. *In* what are they supposed to pay?

as the non-capitalists. These conditions, while formally odd, may be fairly common in practice. None the less, since no valid generalization can be made about the perfectly competitive capitalist group as a whole and discrimination within it would involve an elaborate analysis of cost conditions, it has been thought well to omit in this passage all reference to the behaviour of capitalists in perfect competition. The commodities which they produce are largely the same as those of the non-capitalists.

In the goods produced? In the goods for which those could be exchanged? Some ambiguity was left at that point. It is unnecessary to beat about the bush. What they do pay in is money. This fact introduces a new determinant.

Consider the case of a uniform advance in a capitalist society. We have to ascertain (i) whether there is any rise in the rate of hire for the collaborating factors, (ii) whether there is any diminution in their output per unit, and (iii) whether there is any decrease of elasticity of demand on balance. Suppose that all these changes are in fact registered. Then if the old position was one of equilibrium, the new situation must, it seems, demand a return to it; if marginal revenue was equal to marginal cost before, it must now fall short of it. But no; for suppose in the new situation prices are generally higher. The general level of prices is a notion which is open to and has received much criticism. But in this case the meaning is clear; for a uniform advance of production was defined as one which left unchanged the rates at which the commodities exchanged against one another. If the rate at which one of them exchanges against money goes down, we must suppose all to go down in equal measure, and, in fact, that the general price-level rises in equal measure. If the uniform advance was accompanied by such a rise, the rise might be just sufficient to offset the stabilizing factors. In relation to uniform changes of output the general price-level may and must be regarded as a fourth determinant. Is its behaviour in relation to changes of output such as to entail a stabilizing or de-stabilizing force?

The reader may complain that, whereas he was led to suppose that, as each new facet of our economic system was revealed, an exhaustive list of determinants was kept up to date, yet all this time there was lurking an unnoticed and unmentioned determinant, perhaps a source of disturbance. It may be claimed that he was fairly treated. When reference was made to hiring or paying factors, he was warned that something still had to be cleared up. If in the upshot it had been laid down that factors were paid in kind, the fourth determinant would never have appeared. It only comes into existence when it is postulated that the prime factors are paid in money.

If these factors were paid in money but on a continuously and continually adjustable sliding scale, which made their money payment tantamount to a payment in kind, the fourth determinant would not come into operation. But this method of payment on a sliding scale would not be the same as those sometimes adopted by which rates of wage or salary alter with the cost of living. For the scales actually adopted, apart from the fact that they are not continuously and continually adjusted, do not usually even vary in full and strict proportion to the cost of living; nor, if they did, would they avoid the necessity of introducing a fourth determinant. For that to happen they would have to vary in full proportion either with the value of the product or with the general price-level. And the general price-level cannot be identified with the cost of living of the prime factors, for luxury goods may bulk more largely in the former than the latter, and, more important, the prices of capital goods—though mention of them is strictly taboo in this chapter—have to be taken into account.

The moment has now come when we must take a plunge into strange and unfamiliar waters. So far in reviewing one determinant after another we have been able to rely on our knowledge of human nature, of the known purposes of economic activity reduced to their simplest terms, of certain broad principles amounting almost to truisms, and have deduced what may be expected to happen as the level of activity varies. But in this case it is proposed to ask not what may be expected to happen to the general level of prices as output varies, but what does in fact usually happen. This is a complete change in the method of procedure, and it is important to emphasize very strongly that it is a change.

Why make a troublesome change of method at this point? Is it not likely merely to lead to confusion? The reason is that when we examine the fundamental facts of human nature, when we regard the economic motive in its simplest terms, in order to discover whether prices are likely to rise or fall as activity is increased, nothing whatever is vouchsafed us. When the *a priori* yields nothing, it may be well to revert to observed facts. We have reviewed four determinants in order (subsequently reduced to three for capitalism) and have been able to say what is relevant about each. Now we are faced with a fifth (in future to be called fourth) determinant which may be of first-rate importance. Are we to say nothing and leave the question in the air? This would prove highly inconvenient, when we pass on to the problems of the next chapter. And what can be said by a departure from the method so far laid down may prove not a little useful.

The behaviour of the trade cycle, perverse and obstinate as it is, has provided a great stimulus to those who hope to arrive at general economic laws by observation of the facts. And the trade cycle phenomena have also suggested conclusions to some who, on principle, would scorn such empiricism. The repeated recurrence of certain phases gives a scope for the use of inductive methods otherwise rare in the chop and change of human affairs. It must not be supposed that anything very precise and accurate has been achieved on these lines; only a few rough and tentative generalizations have so far been possible. But nothing in economics is likely to be more fruitful than the work of such as Professor Wesley Mitchell who are making strenuous efforts to extract further empirical generalizations from the observation of trade cycle phenomena. Empirical laws are exceedingly rare in economic studies, and the fact that trade cycle observation has yielded one or two, albeit approximate and tentative, suggests that it is a relatively fertile field for the observer. Those theory-proud writers who belittle such efforts show themselves defective theorists thereby. For who if not the theorist should understand the limitations of theory? Theory divorced from observation is mere definition or tautology. This may be very useful. But the theorist who finds himself able to develop an elaborate structure without the nourishment of more extended observation should at once become self-critical, especially if his conclusions seem to have material significance. He may be sure that material assumptions requiring empirical verification have inserted themselves among his premises. He may pride himself on the demonstrative character of his reasonings and the assured certainty of his conclusions. But their assured certainty will be spurious if they have material content. It is the hall-mark of science—of science, that is, actual and realized, not the science of Aristotelian dreams—that its conclusions do not have demonstrable certainty. Those theorists who seek to make economics more scientific by eschewing the uncertainties, which are necessarily attached to empirical methods, are in fact taking the path which leads away from science to pure scholastic.

There is wide empirical evidence for the proposition that rising prices are associated with increasing activity and falling prices with declining activity. In our experience of the trade cycle the only very notable exception was the failure of prices to rise in the period from 1925 to 1929. Such an exception is highly interesting and cries for special investigation.[1] The general proposition, rough and tentative as it is, may be accepted, with full recognition indeed of its approximate character, for the purposes of our further argument. The evidence is far-reaching, and the proposition has been widely accepted by economists on the strength of it.

Some writers indeed have seemed to imply that it has even greater strength than this—that it is deducible from certain general principles of monetary theory. This, however,

[1] Cp. *infra*, pp. 208–14.

is an illusion. Reasons and explanations can indeed be found for the phenomenon. But without the brute fact to guide them, it is most unlikely that theorists would ever have reached this proposition as a conclusion drawn from general reasoning. On the contrary, they would have been inclined to take the opposite view, for the most general considerations connected with money suggest it. When activity increases, the flow of goods, for exchanging which money acts as the medium, increases more than the quantity of gold (and/or silver) available for the purpose. This is due to the fact that the stocks of metals in use as money comprise not only those concurrently produced, the production of which might well be increased as rapidly as or more rapidly than other commodities, but also the far greater stocks handed down to the present from the past. The most general theory of money suggests that the general level of prices depends upon the relation between the size of the stock of money available for use and the flow of goods which it has to be exchanged against, and that, if the flow of goods increases more rapidly than the stock of metal, as it does in a boom, the price-level should *fall*—a smaller quantity of money being available for exchange against each unit of the commodities. At this point the velocity of circulation is introduced into the argument; general theory does not speak with a very clear voice on this topic, but the most favoured line of reasoning is as follows. If prices are expected to rise, money is regarded as a depreciating asset and will be passed from hand to hand more quickly. Thus the anticipation of a rise in prices causes money to circulate more rapidly; that has the same effect as an increase in its quantity and should, in accordance with general theory, cause prices to rise; and this happens when an increase of productive activity takes place. This argument clearly amounts to nothing. For if, consideration of velocity apart, prices might be expected to fall as goods became more abundant, then the velocity argument indicates that they should fall even more in the boom. At this point the arguments of those who think that prices should be expected to rise as activity increases become more subtle and intricate; they refer to the behaviour of banks and the rate of interest; and doubtless much of what they say is true. But if they imagine that they could have gone through all that maze of deduction and reached this conclusion by the light of pure reason and without the aid of that far greater guiding light, the brute fact that prices do actually rise in booms and fall in slumps, they are most plainly deluding themselves. This fact, that prices rise when goods are turned out in greater abundance and fall in the opposite situation, is a striking paradox and requires to be seen to be believed. It is one of the very few generalizations vouchsafed by empirical observation in economics; and it is probably the best established of any. All the same, it must be used with great caution. There are many minor exceptions. It certainly cannot be stated in the form that whenever a rise of output occurs, prices rise and whenever a fall, prices fall. This is not true. But the correlation is sufficiently close over a sufficiently wide field for us to believe it probable that there is a causal connexion, and consequently to suspect that where the two movements do not occur together there is a counteracting cause. Reservations must be made, however, with regard to phases of the trade cycle; it appears probable that the connexion is less close in certain phases than in others; for instance, in the early stages of recovery we should not expect to find prices rising so confidently as we should expect to find them falling in the early stages of a slump. We should treat the proposition as an hypothesis strongly suggested by observation.

If it is true, the monetary determinant clearly embodies a de-stabilizing force. The restorative effect of the other stabilizers in the case of a downward departure from a given equilibrium might be entirely offset by a sufficient fall in prices, and conversely in the case of an upward departure. Consequently, if prices do tend to fall in the case of a downward departure, that fact constitutes a de-stabilizing force tending to counteract wholly or in part the forces of the stabilizers; conversely, again, if rising prices accompany increasing activity.

We now approach a crucial stage in the argument. The trade cycle does not constitute an alternation of uniform advances and recessions. The deviations from uniformity are large and notable. The reader is reminded that the term uniform has nothing to do with rate of advance; an advance is said to be uniform if the increases in the output of various commodities are such that their relative prices do not change.

But it is a characteristic of the trade cycle that the advances and recessions, though not uniform, are *general* (with the possible exception of agricultural output, already referred to). For the moment we are concerned with the movements in their general character and not with the deviations from uniformity, though these are very interesting and highly relevant to trade cycle study. The general advance (or recession) might be measured by some such device as the following: Mark a point in an n-dimensional manifold of which the co-ordinates represent the quantity of output of each of n commodities at a given point of time in a real system. Through this point draw a graph, the co-ordinates of which represent for every amount of a given commodity the amount of each commodity, which would have to be produced in the real system, in order that the relative prices of all commodities should remain unchanged. Mark a second point in the manifold to represent the actual output in the real system at a second point of time, and find the point on the graph to which this is nearest. The amount of uniform change of output between the two points of time may be represented by the distance of the second from the first point on the graph. The real movement may be regarded as compounded of that amount of uniform movement and the deviation from it. If the fluctuations of any real system were examined from this point of view there is little doubt that they would be found, so far as the uniform factor is concerned, to consist of alternating increases and decreases in the alternating phases of the trade cycle.[1]

With the upward and downward movements of production we have learnt to expect that upward and downward movements in the general price-level will be associated. We may assume that the values of the other three determinants remain constant in the cycle or only move in one direction. They are directly connected with such fundamental matters as the strength of man's desire for goods; attempts to establish a theory of the cycle based on the relation between climate and man's physique having been unsuccessful, it is reasonable to suppose that his fundamental desires and powers are constant within the cycle or only moving in one direction. On this assumption the de-stabilizing influence of money embodied in the ups and downs of prices may be taken to be *a measure of the power of the other three stabilizing forces.*

When we reduced the primitive stabilizers to the terms of their counterparts in a modern capitalistic community, we had some qualms that their ancient vigour might be sadly reduced. The Plasticity of Prime Costs is a broken reed indeed! The Law of Diminishing Returns! These are hardly the days to resurrect Malthus. And a fig for that attenuated, perhaps mythical, entity, the Law of Diminishing Elasticity of Demand. Are these all we have to rely upon? Yet the behaviour of money bears witness that these forces are still stronger than we might be disposed to imagine. For if a given recession is accompanied by a great fall of prices, then the strength of the stabilizing forces supporting the former level of output is precisely measured by the fall of prices that occurs. If there was a temporary equilibrium at the old level and there is now

[1] Cp. R. F. Harrod, 'Imperfect Competition and the Trade Cycle', in the *Review of Economic Statistics*, May, 1936.

another temporary equilibrium at the new, then the forces tending to push back the system from the new one are equal to the force exerted by the drop in prices which keeps it there. The fact that as the system moves up and down there are substantial de-stabilizing price-changes proves that the other determinants exert a substantial stabilizing force. Suppose that, when output is at n units, the other determinants exert no stabilizing or de-stabilizing influence over the lower ranges of output, the system being in neutral equilibrium; that means that as output falls there will be no change in rates of pay to prime factors, no change in their marginal productivity as output recedes, and no increasing elasticity of demand. Then, if a fall in prices occurs, the system will move irretrievably to the position of zero output. If it stops short of that it must be because some stabilizing forces have come into being—wage-rates have fallen, or marginal productivity has increased as output receded, or demand has become more elastic, and sufficiently so to offset the drop in prices. The third condition here mentioned may be put more realistically thus. That the demand becomes more elastic is tantamount to saying that the market so alters that it is no longer worth while for the producer to insist as a condition for production on getting a price as far in excess of marginal cost as he was previously doing.

When prices fall, the sooner the downward movement is called to a halt the more powerful the stabilizing forces must be, that is, the more quickly do they offset the fall in prices. If they can offset the fall in prices, when output recedes a short way, they must be operating more powerfully than if they can only do so after output has receded a long way. And that means the same as saying that if the price-drop accompanying a given recession is observed to be large, that is evidence that the other stabilizing forces are strong. The larger the drop the stronger.

The foregoing conclusion that general price fluctuations measure precisely the force of the three stabilizers depends on the view that business men act in boom and depression in their own interest. They do not always do so. In a system in which there is a large number of producers, it is possible to assume that their errors of judgement cancel each other out on balance. It may be, however, that it is rash to assume this. The circumstances of boom or depression may produce a systematic bias. That they do so is precisely the psychological theory of the cycle. Pessimism is said to prevail in the slump; it is not quite clear which of two contradictory policies pessimism should lead business men to adopt, namely, producing less than they could advantageously market or quoting a lower price than they could advantageously ask; psychological theorists usually assume that the former of these errors is made. If this assumption is correct, the force of the three stabilizers is *pro tanto greater* than that indicated by the monetary measure. A given fall of prices, if judgement was steady, would not by itself cause production to run down as far as it does. If, on the other hand, producers keep prices below what they could advantageously ask, the force of the three stabilizers is less than that indicated by the monetary measure. I am not acquainted with decisive evidence in favour of the view that there is a systematic bias in either direction.

It might also be objected that at any point of time the producer even of concurrently consumable goods has to take the future into account in framing his current output policy. This is true. He may take into account the use which he will have for his plant in future and the reaction of his present price policy on future custom. Very intricate questions are involved. For present purposes it may be taken that these considerations are subsumed under the concepts of marginal cost and elasticity of demand.[1]

It should be observed in passing that money does not provide an extra determinant for independent workers. They are concerned with the rate at which they can

[1] Cf. footnote on p. 51.

exchange their products for the objects of their desire. Uniform changes of price leave them unmoved.[1] This must indeed be modified in so far as they have debts fixed in money. Only to that extent are they concerned with the absolute as distinguished from the relative prices of their products. It is probable that an absolute fall of prices will stimulate them to still further efforts, for, since their residual income after the payment of fixed money charges is smaller, the marginal utility of goods acquired by a given amount of effort is increased.

Recessions and advances are not in fact uniform. Moreover, the values of the determinants and their stabilizing power change from time to time. Consequently the picture given of the behaviour of money is only a first rough approximation to what actually happens. A large recession with a deep depression of prices may be followed by a recovery in which prices do not mount to their former level; this is easily explicable if the values of the determinants have a secular trend favourable to advance, if, for instance, the marginal productivity of the prime factors is increasing whether by inventions operating directly upon them or through an increase of capital equipment.

In the foregoing account money has been made to play a notable part in the trade cycle as the arch-destabilizer. It must not be inferred that we are advocating a 'monetary theory' of the trade cycle. Two views, both consistent with our account, may be taken with regard to the role of money. (i) The first is that money is the original and actuating cause of the cyclical movement; put otherwise this says that the value of the monetary determinant undergoes spontaneous and autonomous variations and that these variations occur alternately in either direction and impart to the general movements of output their cyclical character. (ii) The other view is that money is a

---

[1] Uniform changes of prices would leave capitalist producers unmoved also, if these prices included those of prime factors of production, cp. *supra*, p. 37.

passive accomplice in the generation of the cycle, moving up or down, within certain limits, to suit those forces, still unrevealed, which determine the cyclical movement. On this view no spontaneous changes need be supposed to occur in the value of the monetary determinant; indeed, no changes need be supposed to occur at all. For it is quite consistent with what actually happens to suppose that if only the level of output would stay put, the value of money would not change at all. But when the still un-revealed forces ordain that output shall recede, money is capable of exerting a sufficiently de-stabilizing force to overcome the forces of the stabilizers. In fact, it provides a medium enabling output as a whole to stand, so far as all the determinants so far enumerated are concerned, in a condition of neutral equilibrium. If a recession is to take place, the monetary mechanism does not oppose an ob-stinate resistance but allows prices to drop by whatever amount is required; if an advance is to take place, it allows the requisite rise of prices.

It appears that these two views of money are at the opposite extremes with regard to the importance of money as an active cause of fluctuation. According to the former, money is the prime villain of the piece; according to the latter, its part is utterly subordinate—it does what it is told, puts up no resistance to the worst happening, has no will of its own, is a useful and abject tool. That money does play a villain's part, active or passive, is the fact vouchsafed by experience; for if high prices are connected with high activity and low prices with low activity the effect of the monetary determinant is indubitably de-stabilizing. If, in fact, we found that the opposite was the case, that low prices usually accompanied high output, and conversely, then we should argue that money was a stabilizing force in the system. It is not impossible to imagine a state of affairs in which the Law of *Increasing* Returns operated so strongly throughout as to overcome the plasticity of prime costs and the diminishing elasticity of demand and in which the natural tendency to get into a vicious circle of expansion or contraction was only checked by a tendency for prices to fall as output expanded and to rise as output contracted. Such a state of affairs may yet come about. For the present, on the basis of existing experience of the behaviour of prices, it seems safe to say that there is still some net stabilizing force left in the primitive stabilizers and that money exerts the required de-stabilizing influence to allow fluctuation to take place.

I do not propose to pronounce between the active and passive views of money at this stage or to consider various possible intermediate positions. The former view seems to embody the 'monetary theory' in its strict form. This is a little out of favour at present; not that it is formally impossible or has been decisively disproved by empirical evidence; where everything is still a matter of judgement and conjecture it is permissible to suggest at the outset that the monetary theory in its pure and strict form is rather unplausible.

The conditions embodied in the Quantity Theory of money must, indeed, on any correct view be fulfilled. It appears improbable that the cycle owes its origin to initial fluctuations in the quantity of money. On the side of the precious metals we have a fair measure of stability in their conditions of supply. Thus, if the originating cause is to be found on the side of quantity, suspicion must be directed against the bankers. But it is unplausible to suppose that of their own volition they initiate alternating changes in the quantity of credit. No doubt they do expand and contract from time to time; but this may most naturally be regarded as the result of the pressure upon them alternating in its degrees of intensity. If the complaint is that they do not sufficiently resist that pressure so as to counteract its alternations, well, that is tantamount to assigning to money the role of passive accomplice. If pressure does alternate, the original cause is not to be found in the action of bankers. Why does the pressure alternate?

A more plausible form of the theory that monetary changes are the initiating causes connects them with changes in the velocity of circulation. One version of this may be given as an illustration before we pass on. Velocity of circulation is regarded on this view as a function of the expectations which people entertain with regard to the future course of prices. Expectation of a rise raises velocity, since in the light of this expectation money appears to be a depreciating asset which ought to be passed on as quickly as possible. Conversely, when a fall is expected. But these changes in velocity bring about the expected price-changes. On this view it is not necessary to suppose the successive spontaneous occurrence in alternate order of events having opposite tendency. It is a theory of self-perpetuation, by which it can be shown, so it is claimed, that, once a beginning is made, the cycle must continue. With the expectation of falling prices, velocity moves downward and prices therefore fall. The lowest point of velocity and the price-level is reached when people take the gloomiest view about the future of prices, that is, when the expected fall of prices is greatest. When their views cease getting gloomier and no increase in the rate of fall is expected, velocity and prices become stable; this fact shakes the view that they will continue to fall rapidly. Some people begin to expect a decline in the rate of fall, others may even believe that the fall will go no farther; as soon as views about the future fall pass their gloomiest point, velocity and prices begin to rise. As more and more people change over from pessimism to optimism about the future of prices in the light of the facts, prices rise further; people begin to expect a rise of prices and prices rise further still; this rise must be followed by a fall unless it can continue cumulatively and for ever; for during the later period of rise the behaviour of people is based on the expectation of a rise, and if ever that expectation weakens, behaviour will be readjusted in such a way as to make prices fall; thus every rise must be followed by a fall and every fall by a rise. This view is attractive and convincing and is in rough accordance with observed facts regarding the velocity of circulation. If other causal elements are finally given greater weight in our analysis, it may none the less prove capable of being fitted into the completed picture.

It is time to summarize. The purpose of this chapter has been to clear the ground by taking the simple facts, which we know by introspection and common sense to lead man to engage in economic activity, to sort out these facts, and reduce them into classes of concepts which are applicable to modern society as it is organized at present. Leaving aside minutiae and postponing the important but knotty problem of the relation of the output of capital goods to that of consumable goods, we have reduced the basic human motives in undertaking work in a capitalist society to a list of four determinants. In considering variations in the output of the whole community, as contradistinguished from variations in the output of particular producers, the concept of a uniform variation was used, a variation in the level of output being said to be uniform if it does not cause a change in the relative prices of goods.

The four determinants are as follows: (i) The rates of pay at which prime factors of production can be secured. (ii) The efficiency of the prime factors. (iii) The elasticity of demand for commodities. (iv) The general price-level. All these quantities are averages, in the construction of which there are many pitfalls and difficulties. In the case of independent producers we have in place of (i) and (iv), (*a*) the utility of commodities to them and (*b*) the disutility of work. The third determinant (elasticity of demand) only comes into operation if imperfect competition prevails.

We next asked the question—are the values of each or all of the determinants such as to keep the level of activity stable, so long as those values remain the same? The value of a determinant consisting not of a single magnitude, but of a set of magnitudes, each related to a given level of output, the relations of the members of a set to one another may be expressed in the form of a law or principle. The principle connected with determinant (i) we called the Plasticity of Prime Costs. Provided that rates of pay to prime factors may be expected to be higher for a higher level of output, this principle has some stabilizing force, but it does not appear to have a very great one in the modern world. The principle connected with determinant (ii) is the Law of (Diminishing) Returns. So long as the word Diminishing can truthfully be inserted, the principle is a stabilizer. But in a modern community it is only likely to be of great importance if the level of output is high. And it is possible that at low levels the Law of Increasing Returns prevails. This would have a destabilizing influence. With the third determinant is probably associated a Law of Diminishing Elasticity of Demand; this is a stabilizer and, in the writer's judgement, of greater importance than the other two.[1] The two determinants applicable to independent workers both embody strong stabilizing forces. When we came to the fourth determinant, contemplation of man's inner nature yielded no answer to the question—how is the general level of prices likely to behave in relation to variations of output? We were compelled, therefore, to alter our procedure and ascertain, if possible, what happens in fact. Happily this is a point on which trade cycle experience gives the clearest answer. If that answer may be accepted, the fourth determinant acts as a powerful de-stabilizer.

[1] Mr. W. M. Allen has properly observed that the text does not do sufficient justice to the effect of *anticipations* on present policy. A stabilizing influence on sales will be exerted, when the market weakens, if the firm (i) comes to regard the future as likely to be worse than the present and/or, (ii) believes its future position is best guarded by maintaining present contacts with its customers and is prepared to make present loss at the margin to secure this. The former condition entails that marginal cost, properly computed (cf. footnote on p. 84), drops more than it otherwise would in a recession, the second that demand, reckoning the future into account, becomes more elastic than otherwise. It is possible that the stabilizing influence of the stabilizers, revealed by the monetary measure, is at least as much due to these as to the more direct causes.

Then we took up the point that if we could assume the values of all determinants but one to be constant, or moving in one direction only in the actual course of a trade cycle, their effectiveness as stabilizers or de-stabilizers would be accurately measured by the amount of de-stabilizing or stabilizing work that the other determinant was observed to do in the course of the fluctuation. Now it happens that we can observe roughly the amount of de-stabilizing work that the monetary determinant does during the cycle (by observing the fluctuation in the general level of prices), and it is not unreasonable to suppose, if climatic theories are rejected, that the values of the other three determinants do not themselves oscillate. From this it may legitimately be inferred that the other three stabilizers have still in the modern world considerably more force than one might at first blush be prepared to assign to them.

This force is overcome by the de-stabilizing work of money. Starting from the position that we do not know how money is likely to behave in relation to fluctuations in output, we gather from observation that it does in fact behave in a de-stabilizing way. Concerning the question why it does that and whether the oscillation in money originates on the monetary side or is the result of external pressure on the monetary system we preserve an attitude of complete agnosticism. To that extent our result is negative.

How is it that man's economic activity fluctuates in a way so repugnant to common sense and so contrary to what we are led to expect if we reduce the matter to its simplest terms? The conclusion of this chapter is that we know what allows it to behave in that way. The presence of money capable of oscillating in value allows it. But we do not yet know why it behaves in that way or why the value of money does oscillate. That is the problem for the next chapter.

CHAPTER II

INVESTMENT AND OUTPUT

I. *The Relation*

IT has long been a matter of observation that in the upward phase of the trade cycle, activity in the trades producing durable or capital goods increases more rapidly than that in the trades producing concurrently consumable goods, and conversely in the downward phase. This fact has struck the notice of many writers and has been made the basis of various theories. The National Bureau of Economic Research (U.S.) has been making elaborate studies of trade cycle phenomena over a wide field, and Professor J. M. Clark has given a preliminary survey of the results of these studies in a book entitled *Strategic Factors of Business Cycles*, which is of the highest interest in this connexion.[1] The investigations confirm the generalization mentioned above, which may be regarded as well established.

It is one which of its very nature commands thought and attention. Before letting loose the hounds of theory upon this appetizing morsel, it is well to mention a simple arithmetical relation existing between the demand for concurrently consumable[2] goods and the demand for capital goods, which should be considered in close connexion with the generalization. It is a relation which has, indeed, been noted by learned writers often enough. None the less I have the impression that not nearly sufficient importance has, on the whole, been attached to it. Its simplicity, ineluctability, and independence of all special theories as to the workings of the cyclical process demand

---

[1] Cp. especially pp. 73–9.

[2] In the text the word 'consumable' will be used for short instead of 'concurrently consumable'. It must be understood that consumable goods excludes consumers' capital goods, such as houses. Consumption will refer to the annihilation of concurrently consumable goods together with the *use* of consumers' durable or capital goods.

for it pride of place. It lies at the base of the reasonings which I shall endeavour to advance in the following pages.

The output of capital goods may be divided into two parts, albeit the line of demarcation is not perfectly distinct, namely, (i) that which keeps the existing stock of capital goods intact and (ii) that which serves to increase the existing stock of capital goods. These categories have a loose relation to somewhat different concepts, namely, replacements and net investment, the two together constituting gross investment. The relation is only a loose one, since the three latter concepts include all forms of capital and include therefore stocks of raw materials, consumable goods, &c., as well as 'capital goods' in the narrower sense of fixed aids to production and durable consumers' goods, or of the product of the 'capital goods industries'. Net investment occurs if there is an addition to the stock of consumable goods, even although the quantity of capital goods in the narrow sense remains unchanged. In this essay we shall be mainly concerned with the broader concept of net investment. The relation about to be explained applies both to the broader and the narrower categories.

There is some difficulty in giving a precise definition to the process of keeping capital intact; and this difficulty blurs the line dividing replacements from net investment. In order to give a clear account of the relation between the output of consumable goods and net investment, a simplifying assumption will, albeit very temporarily, be made. Suppose that within certain time-limits changes in the technique of production do not occur and that any advances or recessions in the volume of production and consumption are, so far as the use of capital goods is concerned, neutral. By this I mean that any quantity of output of consumable goods and consumption, added to or subtracted from a given level, requires an amount of extra capital goods of various kinds bearing the same proportion to the existing volume of capital goods of each kind that the increment or decrement of output bears to the given level. Then, (i) in order to maintain output at a given level, replacements of a constant amount are necessary. (ii) In order to increase the output of consumable goods, additional capital goods (net investment) are necessary. The amount of these latter depends on the rate at which consumption is increasing. Thus if consumption were advancing at the rate of two per cent. per annum, only half as much net investment would be necessary as would be required to sustain an advance of 4 per cent. Large changes in the rate of advance of consumption clearly do not entail any great change in the absolute amount of consumption; yet they do entail great changes in the absolute amount of net investment. Mere cessation in the increase of consumption would entail a drop in net investment to zero. And, since net investment is responsible for a large proportion of the activity of capital goods industries, a cessation of the advance of consumption, without any decrease in its absolute amount, would entail a vast falling off in the activity of capital goods industries.

Not all capital goods are required for the physical process of production; some, for example, residential houses, yield their services direct to the consumers. The same principle applies in the cases of these. House building is required to replace houses demolished, and also, the greater part of it, to provide new accommodation. Suppose the accommodation utilized to vary in proportion to the volume of consumption in general. A rise in consumption of 4 per cent. per annum would entail the use of twice as much new accommodation as would be required if the rise were only 2 per cent. per annum. And building activity might be expected to vary very greatly although no large changes were occurring in the absolute amount of consumption.

Gross investment, strictly speaking, includes the whole of production. The whole of output in a given period may be divided into that consumed and the addition to the outstanding volume of capital goods, fixed and circulating (net investment). What is consumed must be replaced if the value of capital goods of all sorts is to be kept intact. Thus replacement plus net investment constitutes the whole of output. But a distinction is necessary between those goods which entirely lose their physical identity and are completely absorbed into the goods consumed, and those which continue year after year assisting the productive process. The former must be completely replaced when consumption occurs. The latter are replaced from time to time; but there is no exact correspondence in the short period between the amount by which they may be conceived to have been used up and the amount of replacement. Moreover, if a fall in consumption occurs this (latter) kind of replacement may come to a complete standstill for a time, since, to begin with, no substitutes need be found for the machines, &c., worn out. It is this (latter) kind of replacement which is particularly related to the activity of the capital goods industries; and in what follows the term replacement will be used to refer to replacement in this narrow sense.

The arithmetical relation just described in and by itself gives a reason why the activity of the capital goods industries might be expected to fluctuate more than that of the consumable goods industries, and may be considered in connexion with the generalization that in fact they do so, which is derived from experience. Moreover, taken in conjunction with another fact, namely, the incomplete mobility of the prime factors of production, it provides the elements of a self-perpetuating theory of the trade cycle.

Suppose at a point of time the level of output to be below what is possible, in the sense that the monetary de-stabilizer could be relied on to overcome the resistance of the three stabilizers over a certain upward range. Suppose an increase of output actually to eventuate. After any outstanding surplus capital plant is brought back into use, the activity of the capital goods trades becomes abnormally high; for a time the increase of general activity is itself above normal, the unemployed being taken into work; this rate of increase cannot be maintained, since, when the slack of unemployment is taken up and the monetary de-stabilizer has exerted all its influence or a great part of its possible influence in raising activity, any further advance must depend on increasing population or improving technique; in the abnormal period the rate of advance depends on these, *and* on the possibility of taking back the unemployed into work. This argument assumes that the slack of unemployed available for reabsorption into work exceeds the surplus plant capacity similarly available at the outset. And rightly. For in the preceding period of low activity plant was not extended at the normal rate and in many cases not kept intact, but the unemployed workers continued to live and the population to increase at the normal rate. Thus, after a low period the initial slack of human unemployment may be expected to exceed that of surplus plant capacity.

When the period of abnormal advance comes to an end, there must be some recession in the capital goods industries. But if the prime factors of production are incompletely mobile and cannot be rapidly absorbed in the consumption goods industries as they are displaced from the capital goods industries, total activity must recede. If the total output, and therefore the total income of the community, falls, it is highly probable that there will be some recession in consumption and therefore in the consumption goods industries. This is the depression. Thus the boom, constituting as it does an abnormally high increase in the output of consumption goods, must on this argument be followed by a depression.

The argument can be extended to show that a revival from depression also is probable. If consumption actually recedes, complete replacement of existing capital goods will not be necessary. Certain replacements and repairs are necessary from time to time to keep a centre of output in operation at all. These might be called 'overhead' replacements. But some are related to the volume of its activity. To give an example in very simple terms, suppose that the machines of a firm last ten years and ten per cent. of these machines are normally replaced each year when the level of output is steady. Suppose a recession in output of 20 per cent.; in the first two years it will not be necessary to replace machines at all; but thereafter replacement must revive. This necessity involves increased activity in the capital goods industry, although no increase of consumption occurs. But if total output and income thus increase, an increase of consumption is highly probable. This is the revival. But if the recovery finally does not merely keep pace with the increase of population, but absorbs some of the unemployed, this is a rate of advance which cannot be permanently maintained. This is the early stage of the boom, and necessarily entails a subsequent depression.

It is now expedient to withdraw the unrealistic assumption made above, that productive methods do not change and that advances and recessions are neutral. This withdrawal will cause us to modify the severity with which we supposed small changes in consumption to operate upon the capital goods industries in accordance with the arithmetical relation which will be called hereafter the 'Relation', but leaves our argument substantially unimpaired.

It has been seen that, on the simplifying assumption, in the event of consumption ceasing to advance, net investment must fall to zero, and in the event of a fall of consumption, replacement for a time will fall very near to zero. It does not seem probable that in fact net investment and gross investment fluctuate quite as much as this; the 'Relation' rather over-explains the facts observed. The reason is that some modifying circumstances have to be noted when we withdraw our simplifying assumption. Net Investment, in addition to that required as a basis of increases of consumption, may also occur because a representative parcel of consumable goods comes to require more capital for its production. This may occur either (i) owing to a fall in the rate of interest which makes capital a relatively cheaper factor of production and so stimulates its use, or (ii) owing to a fall in the relative prices of capital goods compared with those of consumable goods, or (iii) owing to improvements of productive technique requiring a larger use of capital to make the representative parcel, or to changes of taste which alter the representative parcel so that it includes more goods or more of certain goods in the production of which capital plays a big part. Net investment will only occur as a result of (i) if the rate of interest is falling. Changes of the rate of interest are not responsible for the direction of the movements in the relative value of net investment in boom and slump, for they move in the opposite direction to that required. Drawing again from the field of observation, we find interest rates tending to be high in the boom and low in the slump. Thus, so far as the rate of interest is concerned, net investment is discouraged in the boom. And this is right and proper. The stimulus to net investment afforded by the Relation being so great, it is fortunate that we have the rate of interest to provide some counterweight. High rates in the boom and low rates in the slump do something to check the vagaries of net investment which we should otherwise expect. Furthermore, (ii) the relative prices of capital goods tend to be lower in the slump and higher in the boom in relation to general prices, and this should reinforce the fluctuations in the interest rate.[1] In the light of this, which seems clear enough, it is odd to find the view expressed, that the rate of interest behaves in such a way as to make the productive process 'unduly elongated' (i.e. such as to

[1] The reason for this fact is given on p. 77. I am indebted to Mr. Meade for drawing my attention to its significance in this connexion.

require an abnormally large amount of capital per representative parcel produced) in the boom.

(iii) The importance of the third influence on the amount of capital required per unit of goods produced, namely, improvements and inventions, resides not so much in its effect upon the fluctuation as in the fact that it provides a steady basis of net investment, in addition to that varying with the amount of consumption, on which those variations are superimposed.

Inventions occur from time to time making more capitalistic methods of production profitable, and these may be introduced to supersede or assist less mechanical processes whether the level of consumption is advancing, constant, or receding. Along with them may be considered changes, about which it is not certain whether they should be regarded as affecting net investment or only gross investment, namely, all inventions and improvements whether they make the productive process more capitalistic or not. An important invention may occur, making it clearly worth while to scrap existing plant and instal a new one, and this causes an addition to gross investment whether the ratio of capital to the other factors of production per unit of output, required by the new method, is greater or less than that required by the old.[1] Whether this kind of re-equipment involves only an increase of gross investment or an increase of net investment also, depends on the definition of maintaining capital intact. If this requires that plant must not only be kept physically intact, but also brought up-to-date as regards its specific form, whenever it is profitable to do so,

[1] Dr. Simon Kuznets has made an interesting suggestion with regard to how the revival may be assisted, once consumption has begun to increase. New methods may be invented during the slump, the superiority of which is not sufficient to justify the scrapping of old plant, so long as turnover is low, but which can be profitably adopted, as soon as a sufficient increase of turnover takes place, even though existing capacity is still redundant. See *Relation between Capital Goods and Finished Products* in *Economic Essays in honour of Wesley Clair Mitchell*.

then the invention should be regarded as involving net investment, only if it raises the amount of capital required for producing a unit of output.[1] A similar argument applies to alterations in consumers' tastes. These changes prevent net and gross investment falling in a recession to the very low levels suggested by the Relation, and do something to mitigate the fluctuations considered as percentages of total investment, gross or net, which that would otherwise set up.[2]

Whether these inventions are more potent in boom or slump or are equally potent in each is a debatable point. Professor Schumpeter has advanced the view that the boom is essentially characterized and indeed caused by an outcrop of new inventions. There is nothing in his theory inconsistent with what I contend; but, on the other hand, it is not necessary to my argument. That inventions provide the original alternating impetus to the cyclical movement is possible, although there does not seem any readily acceptable reason why they should come by fits and starts; but if some other self-perpetuating theory of the cycle is adopted, it is quite likely that inventions assist the boom, since the environment of optimism and high profits is a favourable one for new experiments involving uncertainty; on the other hand, it is often argued that the distress of entrepreneurs in the depression is a strong force making them seek out and apply new inventions, especially those which reduce costs as contradistinguished from those which suggest opening a new line of product. It is possible to remain agnostic in this matter.

The income of any community in a given period is constituted by its output. Output in any period consists of the goods consumed in that period plus net investment; if saving is defined as the sum of the incomes of every one,

---

[1] For a discussion of this topic see Professor Pigou on Net Income and Capital Depletion (*Economic Journal*, June 1935).

[2] In this paragraph gross investment is used to mean net investment and replacements in the narrow sense explained on p. 56.

including corporate bodies, less what they choose to spend on consumable goods, net investment must be equal to saving. We have seen reason to expect that net investment would constitute a largely fluctuating proportion of total output, and experience bears out that expectation. How is it that the amount which people choose to save constitutes a largely fluctuating proportion of their income? The reverse might naturally be expected to be the case.

A word should be said at this point about replacements. We have seen that it is difficult to draw the line between net investment and the maintenance of capital intact. Since we cannot easily determine what part of the provision of capital goods is required to maintain capital intact, there will be a corresponding ambiguity in the evaluation of net investment and therefore of total output, of which net investment is a part. A similar ambiguity besets the evaluation of total income. Accountants are well aware of the arbitrary nature of the assessment of a firm's profits due to the year's operations; the arbitrariness may, indeed, be due to policy as well as to the difficulties which reside in the nature of the case. If the same principles for defining the maintenance of capital are used in the assessment of output as in the assessment of income, then the value of total output will be equal to that of total income and net investment will be equal to saving.

There are, however, still some difficulties. In evaluating income, what firms set aside for the depreciation of equipment is not included. In evaluating output, the value of replacements is not included, since that value is already counted in the value of the consumable goods produced. It may happen that a firm sets aside for depreciation more than it actually spends in maintenance; this may be perfectly proper, as when a new plant has recently been installed, not needing much expenditure on repairs, and an amortization fund is accumulated to replace it after a lapse of time. Other firms may at the same time be spending more on replacement than they are setting aside for amortization in a given period of assessment. If these excesses and deficiencies cancel out, the matter is a simple one. The amortization fund held against depreciation consists of assets of some kind (money or securities); the firms spending an excess on replacement dispose of assets in which the other firms in a reverse situation invest their amortization funds. Suppose that it happens that the total amount spent by all firms on replacements exceeds the total amount set aside for this purpose in the assessment period. This may occur since a number of renewals may all fall due together. In such an eventuality the excess of expenditure on replacement over that set aside during the period for depreciation should be regarded as net investment. The reader may experience a mental resistance to regarding this as net investment, since it may be that the firms over a longer period are making no net investment at all but are merely maintaining intact the capital goods required for a given amount of output by making replacements at the appropriate time. This is quite true. None the less, it is of the highest interest for the investigation of the cycle to know, if it be the case, that the value of capital goods, assessed by their future power to produce, is being allowed to run down in one period and is increased in another. And it is quite proper to call the increase a net investment. To carry out the work, the firms will have to release cash or borrow from the public either directly by a sale of securities from their reserve portfolio or indirectly through the banks, or they may acquire the means by ploughing in profits concurrently earned. In any of these cases the net investment absorbs a corresponding amount of what people generally, including the firms themselves, are choosing to save.

When firms as a whole are in the opposite position, setting aside more to amortization funds than they are using, a dis-investment is taking place. While this process

of accumulating in excess of replacement expenditure is
going on, it is probable that some firms are engaged in the
construction of wholly new capital goods. The dis-investment by the accumulating firms must be subtracted from
this in order to assess the amount of net investment in the
whole community. It is only this total of new construction so diminished which will draw upon saving from income, for the remainder can be financed out of the
amortization funds of the dis-investing firms, which
must go somewhere. It will be remembered that total
output is found by adding the consumable goods sold
to net investment. Now the value of the goods sold by
the firms, whose amortization funds are accumulating,
exceeds the total they spend in the period, including
replacement expenditure, on the production of those
goods, because they are not actually keeping their own
physical capital intact. Yet in the community as a whole
capital is being kept intact in an indirect way, for some
firms are embarking on new construction. It is quite
proper therefore to subtract the excess of current amortization over current expenditure on replacement from
the value of new construction in order to determine net
investment.

Suppose, finally, that there is no new construction or
insufficient to absorb the excess amortization funds. In
this case there is net dis-investment and dis-saving. If
it is found possible to maintain the amortization funds,
this means that all firms are receiving more from the sale
of consumable goods than they are disbursing as incomes
to the various parties concerned. This can only happen
if the consumers are spending in excess of their incomes.
To do this they sell securities which the firms buy up
for their amortization funds or release cash balances which
the firms absorb. Then the total output is equal to the
value of consumable goods sold less the excess of the
amortization funds over expenditure on replacement, and
total income is equal to the value of consumable goods

bought less dis-saving. Net dis-investment is equal to dis-saving. An apology is due to the reader for this somewhat lengthy excursus.

II. *The Multiplier*

We return to the question how the expected and realized fluctuation in the ratio of net investment to total output in boom and slump is consistent with the ordinary behaviour of individuals with regard to spending and saving. Why should individuals in a boom choose to save such a rapidly rising proportion of their income? If they did not, the boom could not take the form which it does in fact take. The attempt to solve this problem will throw light on the causes of various other characteristic features of boom and slump.

Mr. Keynes has examined this problem very minutely in his Treatise on Money; and in his latest book he has advanced theories which bear closely upon it. I propose to pick out and bring together certain points from each book.

In his Treatise on Money he laid stress on the existence of supernormal and subnormal profit in the boom and slump. (These were called profit and loss, respectively, the condition commonly regarded as one of normal profit being called by him one in which there is neither profit nor loss.) The no-profit (nor loss) condition was defined as one, 'which, if they (the entrepreneurs) were open to make new bargains with all the factors of production at the currently prevailing rates of earnings, would leave them under no motive either to increase or decrease their scale of operations.' Thus profit (supernormal profit) was connected with the boom by definition, since supernormal profit is said to occur whenever entrepreneurs are on balance led to increase output. Boom and slump were considered, rather unsatisfactorily, as lying on either side of a stationary state. (It would have been better had he defined his terms, as he easily might have, so as to make boom and slump lie on either side of a condition of steady advance.) The treatment was unsatisfactory for two more serious reasons. (i) Entrepreneurs were conceived never to be in temporary equilibrium during the processes of boom and slump. (Were they even in temporary equilibrium at the turning-points? Surely not!) They were always behind the times, producing more or less than the current conditions of loss or profit dictated. It is by no means clear that this treatment corresponds with the facts of the case. It is by no means clear that at any and every given point of the boom the representative entrepreneur, if asked whether he now judged that in the immediately preceding period he had produced too little, would answer in the affirmative. Yet that is what the notion that the present level of profit requires him to revise his ideas upwards implies. It is not merely greater prospective profit that, according to this notion, requires him to expand; it is the presence of profit at all; but profit (supernormal profit according to our usage) is present by definition during the boom; this, even if it is not expected to grow, is held to indicate that expansion is right; and this involves that he has been wrong in not producing more than he did for the present occasion. The same arguments apply to this analysis of the recession. (ii) There is no treatment of the marginal position of entrepreneurs; the treatment suggests that the entrepreneur is influenced not by his marginal position, but by the excess of his total receipts over costs. This suggestion, which however is not explicitly developed, is clearly wrong. Very high profit is quite consistent with equilibrium at the margin. Mr. Keynes might then have replied that such high profit would not be profit in his sense. Such a reply would divorce his conception of profit from that profit subject to statistical measurement which is observed to occur in booms; it would involve therefore that his theory accounted for less of the phenomena than it appeared to. And at the

end we might still ask him—well, what does happen to
entrepreneurs generally at the margin in boom and slump?
—and get no answer.

Connected with this treatment of profit, a proposition
of great interest was advanced, namely, that investment
(net investment) was in all conditions and at all times
equal to the saved part of income plus profit. This appears to differ, but in fact only does so in form and not
in substance, from the proposition which we stated earlier,
that net investment must in all conditions and at all times
be equal to saving. The apparent difference is due to the
fact that Mr. Keynes explicitly excluded profit by definition from income. But how if some part of the profit is
not saved but spent? If this happened, it was quite
properly argued, there must be still more profit, entrepreneurial expenditure coming back to entrepreneurs, so
that, however much they spent, the unspent part of profit
would always be equal to the difference between investment and saving.

I wish to lay emphasis on three points connected with
the investment/savings relation defined in the Treatise.

(i) The proposition states clearly, for all to see, albeit
in rather a Pickwickian way, that investment (net investment) must always and necessarily be equal to saving.
This is not a recondite discovery but a truism. But it is
a truism that was tending to be lost sight of in certain
intricate discussions regarding the effect of banking policy.
It is characteristic of economics that truisms have to be
stated rather firmly from time to time to check the
growth of fallacies. Mr. Keynes probably perceived dimly
that the time had come when this or something like it
needed stating plainly. But probably only dimly or half-
consciously. For the proposition which he actually propounded, with much éclat, was exactly the opposite,
namely, that in boom and slump investment is unequal to
savings and that important results ensue. This is quite
in conformity with the ordinary psychological principle

by which, when a man wants to lay particular stress on a word, he substitutes in dreams, or even by error in ordinary speech, its opposite. Not that Mr. Keynes committed any error. For he so defined his terms that what he stated was perfectly correct. It was the emphasis that was inverted. The trouble was that, since he was not yet fully and explicitly conscious of the form of the fallacy which was infecting current doctrine, it was a unique opportunity for the unconscious to play its usual foolish trick.

The result was spectacular, for the guilty fallacy, having hitherto lurked in the obscurity of implicit assumptions, came out into the open. Mr. Keynes had said that investment may exceed saving; well, surely a case in point would be when banks expand credit in making advances to industry. The fact that it had been explained that investment necessarily exceeds saving out of an income defined as excluding profit by the exact amount of that profit that is saved, in fact that investment is equal to saving when all forms of income are counted in, was forgotten or neglected or treated as wrong. Thus the fallacy came to revel naked and unashamed in open public and even claimed the patronage of Mr. Keynes. Thus his unconscious mind has proved in the long run of service, although not without some wastage in foolish controversy, for the fallacy once brought out can easily be demolished. For us the proposition contradictory of the fallacy, namely, the truism that net investment must be equal to saving, is of importance; for, whereas the Relation shows plainly why net investment is abnormally high in the boom, it is the truism which drives us on to ask the very pertinent question—how is it that the amount which people choose to save becomes so abnormally high? In the quest for an answer light will be thrown on the nature of the trade cycle itself.

(ii) Some light on this problem has already been shed by Mr. Keynes in the Treatise. The proposition that, when profit occurs, investment must exceed the saving from a total of income not including that profit, is merely formal. But it is connected with a material point of importance. In the boom income is distributed to different classes in abnormal proportions. The profit earners get more than usual. But the profit earners, being on the whole the wealthy part of the community, are also the big savers.[1] Thus the high proportion of income going to profit would itself account for the higher proportion which saving bears to total income. Moreover, there is, during the boom, a well-founded suspicion that part at least of the high profit cannot be permanent. Its recipients are less likely to raise their standard of living than they would be in the event of an increase of income expected to be permanent; such windfall gains will be largely saved. Again, companies making these swollen profits will distribute a smaller proportion in dividends, being reluctant to have to reduce their rate of dividend at a later stage, will tuck away substantial sums in reserves, visible or hidden, or distribute bonus shares, which the receivers regard as additions to their capital. The whole of the allocation to reserve is saved. Thus this abnormal distribution of income, which occurs in the boom, to some extent explains the high proportion of saving. Similar reasonings apply to the slump.

(iii) The third important point concerns the role of the rate of interest. It might happen that any tendency towards a rising ratio of output of capital goods in accordance with the Relation would be counteracted by a sufficient rise in the rate of interest and a sufficient consequential decrease in the amount of capital goods used per unit of output to preserve the existing ratio. Traditional doctrine has been inclined to take the view that a sufficient rise in the rate of interest, in this sense, may be expected to happen, and that, if it does not, that is due to some temporary disturbance, some time-lag, or some fault in

[1] Cp. note, p. 106.

the monetary system. Yet in fact the movement of the ratio of capital to consumable output is so regularly recurrent and so marked in importance, that these time-lag theories appear somewhat unplausible and unsatisfying. To meet this situation Mr. Keynes advanced a double doctrine, namely, (a) that a sufficient rise in the rate of interest need not happen, and (b) that, except in certain special circumstances, a sufficient rise cannot happen. The second of these propositions arises out of his special theory of what determines the rate of interest, adumbrated in the Treatise and made more explicit in the subsequent volume, with which we are not yet concerned. The first doctrine is connected with the investment/savings theorem and amounts to this, namely, that the rate of interest need not rise as the ratio of capital output increases, because there is a source other than the ordinary saving by people out of their ordinary income from which the required saving may come, viz. supernormal profit.

I propose to single out for reference two doctrines in Mr. Keynes's subsequent volume.

(i) He propounds the view that the general level of economic activity is determined by the amount of investment taking place, in such wise that, given the community's propensity to save, the activity must be just so great as to give people an income from which they will choose to save the amount that is required for that investment. The ratio of the increment of income (= the increment of output) required to make people save an amount equal to the increment of investment is called the Multiplier. It is the contention of this essay that by a study of the interconnexions between the Multiplier and the Relation the secret of the trade cycle may be revealed. The theory of the multiplier implies that the level of activity is not otherwise predetermined and is in accord with doctrines regarding the monetary de-stabilizer already put forward in these pages.

The stress laid on the doctrine of the multiplier involves

some change of emphasis, which is no doubt due to the fact that the recent volume is not primarily concerned with cycle analysis. Instead of varying levels of investment being connected, as previously, with varying levels of profit, they are connected with varying levels of total activity. Instead of increments of investment being financed by savings derived from increments of profit, they are financed from the ordinary savings of the community, the whole level of activity of which is raised, and which therefore has more income to save from. In the first picture the level of output seemed to be frozen; in the second picture little is seen of windfall profit and loss.

Of course, there is nothing discrepant between the two pictures. We may suppose that what actually happens when investment increases is *both* (i) an increase in the general level of activity so that people in general have more income to save from, *and* (ii) a redistribution of income favourable to profit-earners, who are the big savers.

(ii) In the recent volume the marginal analysis comes into its own again. This is an immense improvement. As output expands, prices are conceived to rise owing to the Law of Diminishing Returns operating in the short period. Thus there is no longer any reason to suppose that the price-level diverges during boom and slump in any notable degree from the marginal cost of production (perfect competition) or that the entrepreneurs misjudge their proper course of action throughout the boom and slump. The notion that the level of total profit is the determinant of the entrepreneur's level of activity disappears entirely from view. It should be noticed, however, that the Law of Diminishing Returns provides an incomplete explanation of the rise and fall of prices and that scant attention is paid to conditions of imperfect competition.

An illustration may now be given of the mode of operation of the multiplier. Let us start from a position sketched in the rudimentary outline of a self-perpetuating cycle given in the section on the Relation, namely, when, after a period of low consumption, the rate of replacement must rise if that level of consumption is to be maintained (the beginning of the revival). This, we have already seen, involves an increase of net investment— unless, which is unlikely, the depreciation allocations are simultaneously raised in proportion. So far, however, we have not shown where the increased saving necessary will come from. New net investment begins as soon as those engaged on the replacements begin to earn money. For a few days the whole of the new net investment may be financed by the savings of those who receive that money; before they begin to spend the money they save what they receive. That cannot last for long; the new earners will soon hurry off to the shops and begin to spend that money. The rise of earnings in the capital goods industries will soon lead to an increase of consumption. If this was not anticipated by the consumption goods industries, the stocks of consumption goods will be depleted; this involves dis-investment.[1] At that stage of the proceedings the new net investment will be either wholly offset by a dis-investment consisting in a depletion of the stocks of consumable goods, or partly offset by that dis-investment and for the rest financed by the new savings of the new earners in the capital goods industries. In so far as they do not spend their new income, they save it; the sum of what they save and what they spend (the latter = depletion of consumers' stocks) is equal to the value of the new investment. But the matter clearly does not end there. Those responsible for purveying consumable goods will need to replenish their stocks and will give orders which will entail new employment in the consumable goods industries. It may be noticed in passing that they will probably do more than replenish their stocks, since with the now greater turnover they will feel the need to

---

[1] In the language of certain writers there is at this stage an increase of investment *ex ante*, but no increase or a smaller increase *ex post*.

have larger stocks, and the increase of their stocks above their old level will be an additional net investment. This is an example of the operation of the Relation, bless it, a new net investment in stocks (as well as in other forms of capital) being required by the increase of consumption.

But our main interest for the moment is in the Multiplier. Those newly employed in the consumption goods industries will spend some or all of their earnings on consumption, and there will be a further source of depletion in stocks of consumable goods. These stocks cannot be raised even to their previous levels until sufficient is saved by those newly employed on replacements together with those newly employed in the consumption goods industries—and entrepreneurs will soon begin to touch some new profits also—for the original new net investment in replacements to be financed by that saving. And if some new net investment in consumers' stocks is required as a result of the now-higher level of consumption, the happy spread of employment and increase of income must go on until the volume of new saving is sufficient to finance that new net investment also. The drift into a condition of expansion seems all too easy. The consumption goods industries will soon begin to need still further replacements, and new enterprises may even be started.

The conclusions of this section may be summarized as follows:

1. In any period, however short, net investment is equal to saving.

2. In a short period the amount of investment which those responsible *intend* to make may not be equal to the amount which people choose to save. If the former exceeds the latter, net investment will fall below what was intended owing to a depletion of stocks below the level at which, if developments had been foreseen, they would have been maintained. If the latter exceeds the former, net investment will be above what was intended owing to an undesigned accumulation of stocks. These unintended

changes in the level of stocks must be distinguished from those due to the deliberate action of speculators.

3. These short-period disequilibria, consisting of undesigned changes in the level of stocks, will lead to action intended to rectify matters. If stocks have to be replenished there is a consequent rise in the level of activity and income, and conversely. The amount which people choose to save being directly related to their income level, the effort to replenish stocks, since it raises income, increases the amount which they choose to save, and conversely. Thus, while in the very short period the amount of net investment is determined by the amount which people choose to save, a change in deliberate investment being offset by a change in unintended investment in the opposite direction, in a slightly longer period the amount which people choose to save is determined by the amount of intended net investment, this determination being effected by appropriate variations in the level of the community's income. It is in tracing the effects of this second kind of adjustment with which we shall be mainly concerned. The principle that the amount of saving undertaken is accommodated to the amount of net investment through changes in the level of income is called the doctrine of the multiplier.

4. While changes in the amount of net investment elicit the necessary changes in the amount of saving through variations in total activity and income, it is not to be expected that variations in total income will be fully proportional to variations in net investment and saving. This is owing to two facts: (i) that people tend to save a larger proportion of a larger income, and (ii) that a shift to profit occurs in the boom and a shift away from it in the slump, and profit-earners save a larger proportion of income, especially of increases of income likely to be transitory. Since a larger proportion of income is saved for both these reasons, when income is higher, the proportionate rise in income and output required to elicit a

given proportionate increase of savings need not be as great as the proportionate increase of savings. The existence of the shifts to and from profit is amply vouched for by experience. The theory of imperfect competition makes it possible to provide a more precise explanation of why they occur than has hitherto been given in trade cycle studies, and to this explanation we now proceed.

III. *The Movements of Prices and Profit*

This section[1] is concerned with analysis preliminary to the central part of our theory. Experience, we have already observed, vouchsafes the information that prices tend to rise in the boom and to fall in the slump. We also know that profit does likewise; but the amplitude of profit fluctuation is greater. It is the purpose of what follows to explain the shift of prices and profits in the course of the cycle in a way that is conformable with the general theory of value without introducing hypotheses of time-lags, miscalculations, errors of judgement, or inflation (or deflation) on the part of the banks, &c. The shift to profit is represented as due mainly (i) to the operation of the law of diminishing returns, and (ii) to the diminishing elasticity of demand, as output increases. The reader who is not interested in the details of the analysis and is prepared to take these conclusions on trust may omit this section and proceed to Section IV (the Dynamic Determinants).

In the following argument it will be assumed that entrepreneurs arrange matters in the short period, so far as they can, to make marginal revenue equal to marginal cost.[2] This is the condition for the maximization of profit in any given set of circumstances. Mistakes, of course,

[1] The main points of this section are set out in an article by the writer in the *Review of Economic Statistics*, May 1936.
[2] These should be defined so as to include the repercussions of marginal output on the availability of plant for *future* use, and on the *future* state of the market. (Cf. footnotes on pp. 51 and 84.)

are often made. There may be a systematic bias in the mistakes in certain phases of the cycle; for instance, it will be shown later why orders given for capital goods in the very last phase of the boom must inevitably prove unprofitable. But to suppose that in the short-period decisions how much current output to produce there is systematic error in one direction enduring throughout the whole phase of the boom or the whole phase of the slump by all or most entrepreneurs seems to me altogether far-fetched. If my view be accepted, it can legitimately be assumed that broadly—with minor discrepancies— entrepreneurs do equate marginal revenue to marginal cost in determining the level of current output, and from this certain inferences can be drawn with regard to the observed movements of profits and prices.

I should add, however, that the considerations of this section are not necessary to my main doctrine of the cycle. They are brought forward because they explain certain well-established phenomena in a satisfactory manner. Some may hold that they presuppose too nice a power of calculation on the part of business men. To them my arguments may appear unconvincing; their position is reasonable provided that they do not fall victim to the more superficial explanations which are commonly cur- rent but which are not more likely to be correct because the analysis on which they are based is less exhaustive.

The fluctuation of prices has already been analysed. It measures the force of the three primary stabilizers, viz. the Plasticity of Prime Costs, the Law of Diminishing Returns, and the Law of Diminishing Elasticity of De- mand. If prices are higher in the later phase of the boom, then, on the assumption that business men tend to maxi- mize profit, this must be because rewards to prime factors are higher and/or the marginal physical output of prime factors is lower and/or elasticity of demand is lower. The rise of prices measures the sum of these changes. Some modification of our earlier treatment is due to the fact that we are now placed in a moving world. Total output may increase over a period of time without any pressure for a rise in reward to factors because population is growing. It may do so without the Law of Diminishing Returns operating, or operating so sharply, for the same reason, and also because fixed equipment has increased or improvements have been introduced. It may do so without the elasticity of demand decreasing because population has increased and the rise of total income leaves income per head stationary. These points will be considered.

Not only producers of consumable goods but also producers of capital goods are governed in their level of day to day output by the operation of the four stabilizers. Capital goods, like others, are usually sold to their users; the cost conditions of their producers will obey the same general laws as those in operation in other fields of production; their producers, like others, will try to equate marginal revenue to marginal cost, and, when an advance or recession occurs, we may expect a movement of prices conformable with the action of the three stabilizers. Since, owing to the Relation, the variation in the output of capital goods in boom or slump is greater than that of consumable goods, we may reasonably expect, what in fact we find, that the variation in the price-level of capital goods is greater than the variation in that of consumable goods (except for the produce of the great non-capitalist group).

Profit may increase because the number of goods on which a given profit is made increases. Such an increase is proportional to the increase of output and therefore of income. It does not involve a shift to profit of the kind so useful when a rising ratio of net investment to total output has to be financed. It accounts for a rise of total profit in the boom and a fall in the slump, but it does not account for the observed fact that fluctuations of aggregate profit in the cycle exceed fluctuations of output.

For this to occur, for income to be redistributed in

proportions more favourable to profit in the boom and less favourable in the slump, it is necessary that the percentage rate of profit per unit of output should rise in the boom and fall in the slump. Such changes, and such changes only, are called in the following narrative shifts to and away from profit.

For the investigation of these shifts there is a cardinal principle, namely, that the maximum available profit per unit can only change if one or both of two things happen. Either (i) there must be a change in the relation of the marginal to the average prime cost of production, or (ii) there must be a change in the relation of marginal revenue to price (price must be interpreted as average price where discrimination of prices by a firm among its customers is possible). Profit per unit is equal to the excess of price over average prime cost; but marginal revenue tends to be equated to marginal cost. Therefore, if profit per unit becomes greater or less, either the excess of price over marginal revenue must become greater or less or the difference between marginal cost and average cost must change in the appropriate way. There is no other possibility; this does not depend on any particular theory of the trade cycle but solely on the assumption that the entrepreneur is seeking to maximize profit; the reader would do well to ponder this point and retain it in his mind.

With the aid of this principle we shall examine the movements of prices and profit which occur in the course of fluctuation as a result of the operation of each of the three primary stabilizers in turn. But first we may consider a case in which a shift of profit may be expected to occur without any change in prices. Let us revert to the early stage of recovery discussed in the last section. Replacements are beginning to revive, but the capacity of the general lay-out is still in excess. With this lay-out is loosely connected a minimum cadre of salary- or wage-earning employees, performing functions connected with the general administration, clerical functions, or mere cleaning, door-keeping, &c. The size of this minimum cadre may not be easily variable. None the less, it should be regarded for our purposes as involving prime costs for three reasons.[1] (i) These are costs which could be avoided if operations ceased. They do not in any event enter into marginal cost, and for this reason there may be some mental resistance to regarding them as prime. But though not avoidable in relation to any section of the firm's output, they are avoidable in relation to its whole output. They are incurred concurrently with the decision to undertake output in the short period and not, like capital costs, in advance. (ii) Since the shift to profit assumes importance by reason of the profit-receivers being important savers, whose savings are subject to readier adjustment than those of the prime factors, it is important that this particular section of salary- and wage-earners should be classed with the main body of those, namely, as prime factors. (iii) Changes in rates of pay to prime factors are likely to affect these employees along with the others. For this reason also it is expedient that they should be classed together.

In the early revival output may be increased without a change in the size of this minimum cadre, and the average prime cost will fall on that account. The cost of this minimum cadre could most appropriately be called by the anomalous title of 'overhead primes'. They would certainly be classed for accounting purposes as overheads. In this early stage of revival profit per unit of output may rise without a rise of prices, because it is possible to spread this overhead over a greater number of units.

In the later stages entrepreneurs may get more ambitious and reconstruct their whole lay-out and administrative system with a view to a more grandiose scale of operations. Thus the minimum cadre may grow in number and the overhead that has to be spread may rise. Even

---

[1] The importance of the distinction between variable and invariable prime costs was stressed to me by Dr. Kaldor.

so average prime may continue to fall since greater economies of large-scale production may become possible. The
fall in the average prime which occurs for this reason and
serves to swell profit has no relation to marginal prime
cost. It is consistent with a rise or fall in that. If marginal
cost is stationary over a certain range of increase and this
spread of ₕoverhead⌐is possible, the average prime will
certainly fall. If the marginal cost is rising there is a conflict of forces—but changes in marginal cost are considered
below.

In the recession the average prime cost will, in so far as
it is affected by this 'overhead' factor, tend to rise. There
is an asymmetry here which is worth noticing. In the later
phases of expansion this overhead item may have grown;
it does not follow that it can be reduced in the recession.
The new lay-out and administration are now in being and
will not be reconstructed unless the slump is very severe
and persistent. Thus the fall in profit, *due to this cause*,
when the recession sets in, may be expected to be greater
than the rise in profit due to this cause in the period in
which the increment of output per day, that now has to
be abandoned, was begun. This asymmetry is due to the
irreversible nature of decisions regarding the scale of
capital equipment. It is worth emphasizing, since its
effects correspond with the observed facts of the cycle,
viz. a smaller rise of profit per unit for the last n units of
expansion than the fall of profit per unit for the first n
units of contraction.

It remains to consider the effect on prices and profits
of the operation of the three stabilizers when a fluctuation
in output of a given magnitude takes place.

1. Plasticity of Prime Costs. It will be remembered that
this is the somewhat weakened form in which the Laws of
Diminishing Utility and Increasing Disutility operate in
a capitalist economy. It relates to the variations in the
rates which employers have to pay to the prime factors for
their services per unit. It is not concerned with variations

in the output of prime factors per unit of service paid for, which are looked after by the Law of (Diminishing) Returns.[1] A rise in these rates of pay involving a proportionate rise of marginal costs is associated, *ceteris paribus*, with a rise of prices. Consequently, if these rates of pay do tend to rise with increasing employment or to fall with increasing unemployment, corresponding rises and falls of the price-level in boom and slump may be expected. The fluctuation of prices, however, is usually found to be greater than the fluctuation in money rewards to factors. Thus the operation of the first stabilizer does not account for the whole fluctuation of prices.

The plasticity of prime costs will in general have no tendency to produce a shift to or from profit in a fluctuation in output of a given magnitude. For a change in the rates of reward to prime factors has in general no effect either upon the relation of marginal cost to average cost or upon that of marginal revenue to price, and it is on these relations that the proportion of income going to profit depends. In an economy in which prime costs were more plastic we should expect a greater fluctuation of prices to accompany a given fluctuation of output; but we should not expect a greater shift to or from profit.

This is a paradox which will encounter mental resistance. It may be wiser to ask the reader to reflect upon the demonstration than to burden him with further arguments, which could only repeat it less concisely.

It does not follow that greater plasticity of prime costs would not be a good thing. That depends on the view that is taken about the determination of the price-level. Those who believe that the price-level is an autonomous factor in the situation, determined, for instance, by the decision of bankers, might argue that since the changes in the price-

---

[1] As was noted on p. 29 of ch. i, the factor included in that chapter under the head of Plasticity of Prime Costs, namely, the necessity of taking on less efficient workers, as output expands, is hereafter considered under the head of Diminishing Returns.

level are known and given, if prime costs were more plastic, the variations of output associated with those given changes would be smaller. Those who regard the monetary system as a neutralizing medium accommodating itself to the other factors, which determine the level of output, will not attach weight to this argument. Further discussion is out of place pending the enunciation of our constructive theory of the cycle.

The afore-mentioned paradox may be made more acute by reference to the division of profit between debenture holders and others who have fixed money claims on the one hand and residual profit-earners on the other. Plasticity of prime costs does not affect the shift to and from profit as a whole which occurs in connexion with a given fluctuation of output. But by rendering the price-level more variable it might be expected to alter the distribution between the two sub-classes. In a slump residual profit, that is, profit in the ordinary sense, would be still more squeezed if wages were reduced, and conversely.

It must be noted that in the whole discussion regarding the shift, profit is taken in the broader sense. This follows from the main classification of producers into the prime factors and the profit-earning factors, the latter being all the owners of durable appliances whatever the precise nature of their titles. This classification is particularly convenient in the discussion of this section, since rentiers and entrepreneurs are alike big savers, and we are therefore more concerned with what happens to their joint than to their several incomes.

2. The Law of (Diminishing) Returns. Under this head a rise of output is associated with a rise of prices if marginal costs are on balance rising; it is associated with a shift to profit if the ratio of the marginal costs to average prime costs is rising.

What should we expect to happen to marginal costs in the boom? The Law of Diminishing Returns derived its main force from considerations regarding the powers of the soil. But the soil is largely looked after by non-capitalist producers whose reaction in boom and slump, already considered in the first chapter, is quite different from that of capitalists, and we are not dealing with it here. But in the first chapter it was also pointed out that in capitalist society the Law comes to some extent into its own again in a different way owing to the amount of capital goods in their various specific forms being limited. In the early stages of recovery the Law is probably not operative, since there is surplus capacity. But even in later stages it is doubtful if shortage of specific capital goods plays an important part. This is a point at which the fact that we are dealing with a movement over a period of time becomes significant. In the first chapter we were concerned with different possible levels of output at a particular point of time. Now we are living in a more spacious world. Capital goods can be and are increased in the course of the boom. It is not clear that at any point marginal returns to prime factors fall in a marked degree owing to the shortage of capital goods. Nor is it clear that when the recession sets in marginal returns to prime factors increase very greatly. In this capital equipment is unlike the land. Marginal costs on land may be reduced by cultivating less intensively. But a plant designed for a certain output does not welcome light cultivation. On the contrary, as the operation of a factory is reduced well below capacity, marginal costs may even rise. When, however, production has to expand at a really rapid pace, as in war time, the shortage of capital goods may become important; this may be a leading cause of the quite abnormal rise of prices and profits on such occasions.

In the normal cycle the human factor is much more important. As output increases duds may be taken on in various capacities from top to bottom of the organization, especially if unemployment is falling to a low level. In the later phases this may be quite a notable cause of the rise of prices and the shift to profit. Corresponding falls may be expected in the early phases of the slump.[1]

What is the relation between the changes of marginal cost here considered and the shift to and from profit? A general statement is not possible. But in the majority of relevant cases it appears that a rise in marginal cost should be accompanied by a shift to profit. If marginal cost lies below average prime cost, a rise in marginal cost necessarily raises the ratio of marginal to average prime cost and is thus associated with a shift to profit. This is also necessarily the case if marginal cost exceeds the average prime by less than a given amount; the matter only becomes doubtful, if the marginal cost is greatly in excess of the average prime, and this condition would appear to be exceptional. Thus it appears probable that, when the Law of Diminishing Returns operates, it accounts both for a rise of prices and a shift to profit.

In the long period there may well be a secular upward trend in Returns, whether owing to improvements directly raising the efficiency of the prime factors of production or to an increase in the amount of capital per head. If this is so, a secular downward trend of prices is to be expected, on which the cyclical fluctuations here discussed are super-

[1] Mr. Keynes has developed the amphibian concept of 'User Cost', to which he attaches importance. This is the reduction in the serviceability of plant owing to its use on a particular occasion, which would not have occurred, owing to the mere passage of time, had the plant not been used. Thus it enters into the entrepreneur's short-term calculations as part of the marginal cost which must be covered by marginal revenue, and it is in that sense prime; but it does not represent any concurrent outlay upon factors of production, and is in that sense not prime. Considered as a function of the present level of production, marginal user cost must rise with increasing output, for, whatever happens in future, there are more chances of one unimpaired machine having a given value at a certain future date than there are of two each having that value, &c. Thus User Cost is an additional stabilizer. User Cost is also a function of what is expected to happen; an improvement of prospects makes it probable that any given unimpaired machine will in the future have a greater value than it would otherwise have done, and the cost of impairing it is *pro tanto* greater. Thus a proper estimate of User Cost may make marginal costs fluctuate more than they would on first sight appear to.

imposed. It must be observed, however, that there may also be a secular upward trend in the money rates of payment demanded by prime factors of production, which might partly or wholly offset their increase of efficiency, in which case the secular fall of prices would be *pro tanto* diminished or eliminated.

3. There is one remaining influence affecting the shift to profit as well as the price-level, namely, the elasticity of demand (third stabilizer). Some theoretical considerations were advanced in the first chapter for supposing a Law of Diminishing Elasticity to exist. The behaviour of prices and profits in boom and slump are strong evidence for it. For in neither case do the other relations, already considered, seem sufficient to account for the whole of the movements observed. And our list of governing considerations is exhaustive. In the case of prices, we have the movements in the rates of reward to prime factors and Diminishing Returns at the margin; it is notorious that the movements in the general level of prices considerably exceed the former of these; can we suppose that the Law of Diminishing Returns acts so strongly as to account for the whole excess of the movement of price over the movement of rewards? It seems hardly probable. Particularly is this so in the slump, when, after the first weeding out of inefficients, we can scarcely suppose marginal returns to increase in any very marked manner. It appears that a large amount of the price-drop is still to be accounted for.

The case with profit is similar. Here changes of reward to prime factors do not come into play (except via shifts between the debenture and equity elements in profits); on the other hand, affecting profits but not prices, we have the fall in the average primes owing to the greater spread of invariable primes. Observation suggests that the variation in profit per unit is much larger than that in the price-level. The changing elasticity of demand, if its operation is an important factor, gives us precisely the results we seek. It might account for quite substantial changes in profits and prices, and it would produce larger changes in profit per unit than in the price-level. I give an example. Suppose for simplicity that, on the average, marginal is equal to average prime cost. Suppose the average elasticity of demand confronting all entrepreneurs to be initially 4, which would entail an average profit (including allocations to amortization) on prime expenses of $33\frac{1}{3}$ per cent. Suppose this average elasticity to rise in a recession to 5. This would entail a fall in prices of $6\frac{1}{4}$ per cent. and in profit of 25 per cent. This is the kind of relative change which does occur.[1]

Moreover, changes in elasticity account naturally for the change in price per unit and profit per unit for every unit change of output, being greater in the early phase of the slump than at other times. Economists are too apt to think of the search for the cheapest market as a continuous and all-pervasive process. That is, in fact, only true of dealers in an organized market, of Ricardo in the money market. For others, whether consumers or producing firms, the search for cheapness entails special efforts made on special occasions. During the growing affluence of the boom habits become hardened, part of the extra means are taken out in the wastage due to not bothering too much. When incomes begin to fall people are forced to economize; cherished habits have to be abandoned willy-nilly. At this point they are shaken out of their lethargy; they begin to sit up and take notice. They resent and resist the curtailment of their wonted pleasures and become willing to

---

[1] Elasticity of demand is measured by the expression $\dfrac{y}{x}, \dfrac{dx}{dy}$, where y is the price and x the amount demanded, considered as a function of price. If η stands for elasticity, the relation of the marginal revenue ($=$ marginal cost), z, to price is shown by the equation

$$z = \frac{y(\eta-1)}{\eta}.$$

We can thus compute the change of price and of profit per unit due to a change of elasticity, assuming cost, and therefore z, constant.

take great pains to seek ways and means for mitigating their hardships. Their efforts to find cheapness become strenuous and eager. Nor are commercial firms exempt from this influence upon their purchase policy; they, too, have received a nasty jolt and must strain every nerve to reduce costs. Assurances become widely current in the slump that firms are making special and extraordinary efforts to reduce costs; there is no reason to suppose that these are empty. It is not unreasonable to suppose that entrepreneurs, faced with bankruptcy as they often are, devote quite unusual attention to this subject.

Reverting to the long period, it seems not unreasonable to suppose that, with growing affluence, there is a secular tendency for elasticity of demand to decrease. This is an influence which should be carefully considered by writers who are debating the advantage of long-run policies of stable and falling prices. In and by itself the declining elasticity requires rising prices if a continued advance is to be maintained. The evidence given by the cycle suggesting that changing elasticity of demand is an important factor should endue with caution those who would hastily dismiss this matter as trivial. It is quite possible that the secular trend of elasticity is larger than the secular increase of prime factor efficiency; and, in this case, a long-period upward movement of prices is required if an advance is to be maintained.

The burden of the argument in this section has been that the shift to and from profit is connected with very deeply rooted conditions in our economic system. It is too often treated in a superficial way as due to some temporary lag or some careless misdemeanour. The banks behave improperly with regard to credit; the wage-earners fail to press for a timely rise of wages. I have connected it with the relation of average to marginal costs of production and with the behaviour of elasticity of demand, matters not easily tampered with. It is here represented as necessarily connected with a change in the level of output, not merely as a motive for it, but as its ineluctable consequence.

IV. *The Three Dynamic Determinants*

All references to time-intervals in this topic are highly dangerous; it is so easy to give plausible explanations on the basis of a time-lag hypothesis; the hypotheses that may be introduced are so many and various that with their aid the facts can be made to fit almost any theory; it is extremely difficult to demonstrate that one hypothesis is more probable than another. Yet the fact that net investment is undertaken with a view to facilitating production in the future is clearly a central one; and the interval that elapses between placing an order for, or beginning to undertake the construction of, capital goods and their use in the productive process can hardly be neglected.

Who places such an order gives a hostage to fortune; his judgement can only be vindicated after the interval has elapsed. At any point of time the net investment in progress is due to the sum of orders given in the past but not yet completed. It may be well to make two highly unrealistic assumptions, the utility and shortcomings of which are so patent as to render them innocuous, (i) that orders are homogeneous in the sense that in each short period, say, a day, all firms give orders for a uniform[1] amount of capital for their own purposes, which may be great or small, and (ii) that the net investment due to a given order is the same on every day from its issue to its completion. In that case whether the net investment on a given day is higher or lower than on the previous day depends on whether the new orders given exceed or fall short of the orders completed.

Orders are given on the strength (i) of recent experience and (ii) of guess-work with regard to the future.

---

[1] Uniform relatively to those given by other producers, i.e. designed to produce increments of goods such that their price ratios remain constant. Cp. definition of uniform advance, pp. 14–15.

1. The most recent experience is the use to which the available capital was put on the day prior to the given day. On the given day new orders are lodged and also new capital goods are standing ready for use. The amount of use made of all available capital goods, including those newly ready, depends on the effect of the new investment, working through the multiplier, on the general level of activity on the given day. In reality the level of activity related to a given amount of investment is not accurately determined in any space of time so short as a calendar day owing to the unforeseen variation in the level of stocks.[1] But it will be appreciated that the period of time for which this analysis is really designed is longer than a day, and the following arguments should be considered with that in mind. For the purpose of this analysis we shall take as our starting-point a condition in which a steady advance is in progress. A steady advance is defined as one in which the ratio of the increment of output to the previous level is constant; this involves a geometrical series. It follows that the proportionate increase of net investment on the given day over net investment on the day preceding is equal to the proportionate addition to the stock of capital goods available for use on the given day. The experience of the given day will be the primary test as to whether the advance is likely to remain steady.

Consumption on the given day will increase, for there is an increase of net investment. How much consumption increases depends on three considerations. These three considerations are deduced from the whole of the preceding analysis and occupy the central position in the trade cycle theory of this volume. They may be called the three dynamic determinants, as contradistinguished from those four determinants that have been so often referred to already, which may be called the static determinants. They are dynamic because they determine the rate of growth of output, whereas the static determinants relate

[1] *Vide supra*, pp. 72–4.

to the level of output at a particular point of time. The three primary static determinants prescribe what value of the fourth, namely, the price-level, is consistent with any given level of output in given circumstances.

The three dynamic determinants are (i) the relation of the proportion of the increment of a representative man's income saved to the proportion of the previous total of income that was saved, (ii) the shift to profit connected with a given advance of output, and (iii) the relation of the amount of capital per unit of output involved by the method of production, for which the newly forthcoming capital goods are designed, to the amount of capital per unit of output for which the pre-existent capital goods were designed. These may be named shortly (i) propensity to save, (ii) shift to profit, and (iii) amount of capital used in production.

As a preliminary to further explanation it may be well to state a way in which these three determinants might behave for the steady rate of advance to be justified by the experience of the given day. (i) Suppose that representative income-receivers save the same proportion of their increment of income as they previously saved of the income of the day before.[1] (ii) Suppose that there is no shift to profit. (iii) Suppose that the productive methods for which the new capital goods were designed are the same as those previously employed. On these conditions consumption on the present day will rise in the same proportion as capital goods are increased and by the same amount as that which the new capital goods were designed to provide, and this experience seems to justify the present rate of advance.

That this is so may easily be seen. Conditions (i) and (ii) entail that the value of the multiplier is the same as

---

[1] The use of the concept representative income-receiver is necessary in order to isolate the forces governing the shift to profit. Otherwise the first and second dynamic determinants might be lumped together as proportion of income saved.

previously. Therefore consumption will increase in the same proportion as net investment increases, that is, in the same proportion as the stock of capital goods increases. Condition (iii) entails that if output increases by that amount, it will increase by the amount for which the new capital goods were designed.

If people saved a larger proportion of their increment of income or there were a shift to profit on the given day, the value of the multiplier would fall below its previous level, and, so far as these two determinants were concerned, consumption would advance less than the capital goods increased on the given day. If the new capital goods were designed for more highly capitalistic methods than those previously used (i.e. for methods involving more capital per unit of output), then the increase of output on the given day would, so far as this determinant was concerned, exceed that for which the new capital goods were designed. Thus, in a condition of steady advance a rise in the proportion of income saved or a shift to profit will entail *pro tanto* that the orders maturing in new capital goods on the given day were not fully justified, since the advance in consumption will not be fully proportional to the increase in capital goods available to provide for it. If the new goods are of a more capitalistic design, *pro tanto* the advance of output will exceed that for which they were designed.[1] It is clear that whether the original lodgement of the orders is to be in fact justified on the given day depends on the balance of these considerations. If the previous orders now maturing prove over-justified on the

[1] The reader may have some difficulty here. The assumption is that the new capital goods involve an increase of total capital goods by, say, p per cent. If the new design involves the use of more capital goods per unit of output, output is expected to rise by less than p per cent. But the increase of net investment being p per cent, consumption will rise by p per cent. (on the assumption that the other two determinants are neutral), that is, by more than the new capital was designed to provide for. A method of production is said to be more capitalistic, i.e. to involve the use of more capital goods per unit of output, if, *at a given rate of interest* on the capital goods, the interest charge per unit of output is higher.

given day, then on the basis of the most recent experience the rate at which new orders for capital goods, and so of new net investment, is increased is likely to rise. Conversely, if the previous orders now maturing do not prove fully justified. Thus, so far as recent experience is concerned, these three considerations comprise all the forces determining whether the existing steady rate of advance is to be increased, maintained, or diminished. How are the dynamic determinants likely in fact to behave?

(i) There is reason to believe that people tend to save a larger proportion of a higher income. Some theoretical considerations regarding the probable behaviour of savers are collected in a note appended to this chapter. If this is so, the first dynamic determinant exerts a restrictive influence.[1]

(ii) The shift to profit has been shown in Section III to depend on two factors, (a) increase in the ratio of Marginal to Average prime cost, and (b) the Diminishing Elasticity of Demand. It would be rash to say much a priori about the operation of either of these laws. But experience is that there usually is a shift to profit in a pronounced upward movement, or, what is the same thing, a rise of prices in relation to average prime costs of production. The greater the shift to profit, the smaller the increase of consumption entailed, in accordance with the multiplier, by the given increase of net investment, and the more likely is the existing rate of increase of capital goods to be found to be excessive. This is certainly a striking paradox, since high profit is usually supposed to be the signal for headlong advance. But the reasoning on which it is based seems to be irrefutable. It could only be disputed by a denial of the view that a larger proportion of high profit than of general income tends to be saved.

---

[1] If it were not so and people tended to save a smaller proportion of large incomes, the general character of the argument of the text would not be affected. But the first dynamic determinant would have to be regarded as a force making in general for expansion.

Moreover, it accords with the observed fact that a spectacular accumulation of profit occurs only in the later phase of the boom, that is, shortly precedes a break in that boom. That is a matter of common observation and frequent comment. But though there is always much wise head-shaking and prophetic warning of disaster, couched in the most persuasive language of the pulpit, I do not recollect having seen any rational explanation of why one may be expected to follow from the other. The foregoing argument claims to provide such a rational explanation.

(iii) Inventions often occur to increase the amount of capital required per unit of output. There are some reasons, mentioned on pp. 102–3, for supposing that the importance of this aspect of inventions is a declining one. If that is so, we may find increasing difficulty in securing an advance commensurate with the growing productive power of the working population. Be that as it may, we may suppose that there is some net movement of this kind. More capitalistic methods of production may also be induced by a fall in the rate of interest. The opportunity for bringing them into action is when new capital goods are ordered, and so we have some reason for expecting that the amount of goods per unit of capital, which the new capital is designed to produce, will on balance be less than that for which the old is designed.

Reference has been made in recent literature to an alleged tendency for productive methods to become more capitalistic at a greater rate in the boom than at other times. Is this tendency a real one? It has already been argued in the text (p. 59) that it is difficult to suppose so, owing to the fact that interest rates are apt to be higher, and thus more discouraging to capitalistic methods, in the boom than in the slump. The foregoing argument suggests that none the less the tendency may be a real one. For it is new investment which provides the opportunity for more capitalistic methods to be introduced. And the rate at which methods become more capitalistic may well be higher in the boom, simply because more investment is going on. But it cannot be conceded that methods tend to become *unduly* capitalistic in the boom, or more capitalistic than is suitable for slump conditions; for that would be inconsistent with the observed behaviour of interest rates, as also with the behaviour of the price-level of capital goods in relation to that of goods generally. What probably happens is that, while the rate at which production as a whole becomes more capitalistic is higher in the boom, just because there is more replacement and new investment going on, the amount by which methods of production become more capitalistic per unit of new investment is *less* in the boom than in the slump. In other words, the amount by which each new unit of investment makes the productive process more capitalistic probably tends to be less in the boom. The view that the slump is in any way due to the fact that methods of production become inappropriately capitalistic in the boom, or more capitalistic than is appropriate in subsequent conditions, must be altogether rejected.

This tendency of production to become more capitalistic will offset the restrictive influence of the first two determinants. If the tendency were of constant operation in time, then the net effect of the dynamic determinants would vary with variations in the effects of the first two. But Professor Schumpeter's view that new ideas, the opportunity for exploiting which comes with the onset of the boom, get used up after a time is relevant here. There is reason to suppose that the shift to profit is intensified as the advance continues and available human material is used up. If this is so, the point will come when a given rate of increase of net investment proves no longer justified. This happens as soon as the restrictive force of the first two determinants comes to exceed the expansive force of the third. This is the theory of the boom.

If on the given day the restrictive force of the first two determinants rises for the first time above the expansive force of the third, available capital equipment will not be fully utilized, that is, it will not be utilized as fully as was intended, when it was ordered, for the production of current output. There is disappointment. This suggests a slowing down in the rate of increase of orders for new equipment. In the real world all firms do not order new capital goods every day. The day is, in any case, a quite unrealistically short period to take as that the experience in which forms the basis of policy in ordering capital goods. Be that period what it may. What actually happens in the day, or period, in which the new orders for investment cease to increase at the given rate is that the increase in the number of firms in a position to give orders or the rise of the orders of those, who are giving new orders on that day, goes down.

What is the effect on the situation on the next day? The amount of capital goods coming into existence is not yet affected by the decline in the rate of increase of orders. But the general level of consumption is affected, since the rate of increase of net investment has begun to decline. On the next day there will be a twofold disappointment, (i) owing to the continued operation of the restrictive force of the three dynamic determinants, and (ii) owing to the decline of the rate of increase of net investment, which, in accordance with the operation of the multiplier, causes on its own account the increase of consumption to fall still farther below the increase, for which the forthcoming new capital was designed to provide.

2. Now is the moment to bring into account the second force determining the amount of net investment, viz. guesswork about the future. So far we have been dealing with the effect of realized experience on net investment. Might not the turn of events on the crucial given day have been anticipated, it will be asked, and the decline of net investment have begun not on that day but on the day on which the orders maturing on that day were placed? It might. But in a certain sense in this field correct

anticipation is in principle impossible. For, if the decline
of net investment had begun in anticipation of the turn of
events on the given day, say six months earlier, disappointment, too, would have come six months earlier. However the dynamic determinants are behaving, the decline in
the rate of increase of net investment will bring disappointment on the following day, in consequence of the decline in
consumption in accordance with the operation of the multiplier. This being so, any interruption in the steady advance
of investment orders will be immediately justified by the
results, and it will always be justified *too soon*, viz. when
previous orders are still maturing. This is a notorious phenomenon of the boom, and here receives its theoretical explanation. Since, so far as this effect is concerned, any day is
as good as another for breaking off the advance in net investment, there is no reason to suppose that it is more probable
at one time than another. So long as investment is bravely
maintained it will be justified by results, if the dynamic
determinants are behaving properly. It is only when these
begin to reduce the volume of consumption and output
below the level, which a steady advance requires, that disappointment is bound to occur, whether the capitalists
continue bravely giving hostages to fortune or not. It is
the operation of the dynamic determinants which provides
a material check to expansion, and it is our analysis of them
which raises our theory above the level of a purely psychological one. Whether entrepreneurs wait for the actual
day on which the evil effect of their working is felt before
reducing orders, or whether they anticipate that day by
the full gestation period of orders, and so precipitate the
end of the boom, is a minor matter. It is most unlikely
that they will guess rightly, and experience seems to suggest
that they do not. The condition of psychological optimism
prevalent in a boom may be cited to reinforce this opinion.
But I attach no importance to the arguments either way
on that score. What is clear is that, however the entrepreneurs guess or whatever their degree of optimism, the

operation of the determinants is likely sooner or later to provide a material reason for restriction; and also that, however prudent they are, the falling off in output will come before they anticipated it.

It never rains but it pours. We have not yet traced out the evil consequences of the evil day. We have seen that there will be a twofold evil on the second day. But that is not the end of the matter. When the rate of increase of consumption begins to slow down, what is required in net investment is not merely a slowing down in its rate of increase but a decrease. This is due to the nature of the Relation. Once the implications of the situation are appreciated this must occur. But this will give a nasty shock to the level of income; for if net investment is to decline, the level of income and consumption must do so too (the Multiplier). When consumption falls the level of investment will be rapidly reduced to that required for the more capitalistic character of replacements only (the Relation). Additional capital goods will not be required. The rate of interest is apt to fall in the slump (*vide* the next chapter), and this stimulates a transition to more capitalistic methods, when possible, and so assists in maintaining some net investment. There is a strong shift away from profit, which prevents the Multiplier from reducing consumption too severely. But if the situation were sufficiently bad and, owing to the fall in consumption, not much replacement were required, net investment might well be reduced to zero, any propensity to save on the part of income-receivers in general being offset by unavoidable entrepreneurial losses. However skilfully they equate marginal revenue to marginal cost, many entrepreneurs may be unable to make receipts exceed prime costs by enough to meet the claims of the debenture element: they continue in business, often quite justifiably, in the hope of better days. It would be a pity to dispose of good capital assets.[1] Thus the conjoint action of the Relation

[1] This notion of entrepreneurs continuing in business while making a

and the Multiplier accounts for the catastrophic nature of the slump when it comes.

The sudden and dramatic turn of events at the top of the boom is in marked contrast to the slow and gentle nature of the revival. This contrast calls for a rational explanation; such an explanation is hard to find in those writers who lay stress on the ups and downs of optimism and pessimism, on the rise and fall of prices, on movements in the rate of interest. It is true that in describing the later phases of the boom they use all their literary devices to produce tension and a sense of impending doom in the reader's mind; he is worked up into a condition of taut anxiety, the atmosphere is thundery, and, when a great denouement occurs, he is not surprised. It all seems natural; it is what he was led to anticipate. But as the depression wears on the style takes a marked turn for the placid and soothing. Little by little this and that begin to happen. The gentle ripples of a summer sea push slowly but certainly up the shore. The reader is reminded of the devastating attack of a fever and the pleasant days of convalescence. But this is not science.

To recapitulate this central part of the theory. As soon as disappointment in the results of past investment occurs or is anticipated in consequence of the working of the three dynamic determinants, the rate of increase of investment slows down. This, in accordance with the Multiplier, entails a further slowing down in the rate of increase of consumption. This, in accordance with the Relation, entails an absolute fall in net investment. This, in accordance with the Multiplier, entails an absolute fall in income and consumption. This, in accordance with the Relation, entails that net investment is rapidly reduced to a very low level, if not to zero.

The recession is rapid, but not perhaps so rapid as our

---

loss has nothing to do with any failure to equate marginal revenue to marginal cost. If they continue to work at a loss, they will try to minimize the loss, and that equation is the condition for their doing so.

argument suggests. For, whereas the recovery is a steady
or accelerating climb, our arguments give no reason why
the path to the bottom of the slump should not be quite
precipitous. Some reasons why this is not in fact so may
be thrown out. (i) Some net investment is temporarily
sustained by the existence of outstanding orders, although
what a learned American volume calls the disease of can-
celitis may break out. Thus production will continue to
be held above its lowest level for the whole of the gestation
period. (ii) Advances and recessions are not uniform.
Every industry and every district has its own special
circumstances, and this heterogeneity may do something
to even things out in the community as a whole. (iii) Our
old friends, the non-capitalist producers, may be brought
back into the picture at this point. They continue working
hard, but between them and the consuming public stands
a body of dealers or middlemen, with a point of view of
their own, who struggle to arrest the precipitate decline of
agricultural prices. In order to achieve this they are inclined to let stocks accumulate; but such an accumulation
constitutes net investment and retards the general recession. Thus if the hard-working agriculturists have their
use in being willing to provide an impoverished world
with cheap food, so, too, have the agricultural middlemen who in the worst hour provide a vent for savings
and thus help to limit the recession of general output.
Those who regard the restriction of agricultural output in
a slump as a panacea would do well to bear these points
in mind.[1]

The casual observer may regard the slump as a tacit
conspiracy of people not to take in each other's washing;
and there does not seem on the face of it any reason why it
should not reach its logical conclusion of zero output.
Those who stress the function of pessimism in a slump

[1] This is not to say that planned agricultural restriction may not be
desirable, not, indeed, in the face of a slump, but generally to meet a
secular tendency to relative agricultural over-production.

may well cherish a secret fear that the pessimism will be
cumulative, each individual being justified in the decision
not to produce by the decision of the others. Yet there is
a bottom, or, anyhow, there has been one on all past
occasions.

So long as there is some output, some replacement is
necessary; this may give an opportunity for introducing
more capitalistic methods. Moreover, inventions and improvements proceed—and, indeed, are diligently sought for
by desperate entrepreneurs—and these may make it worth
while to scrap existing plant even before its pre-ordained
term. Happily the rate of interest is inclined to fall in the
slump and this may stimulate the process of substituting
more capitalistic methods. Not that we can legitimately
suppose that all these forms of investment taken together
are as great as the amortization funds would be if they
were properly maintained. And if these forms of investment were not greater than the total of the amortization
funds there would be no net investment. But it may well
prove impossible properly to maintain the amortization
funds for the simple reason that the shift away from profit
has been too great. The magnitude which shrinks in a
recession in accordance with the arguments of Section
III is the excess of receipts over prime costs and includes
amortization funds as well as profit. As this shrinkage
occurs, the shareholder should be sacrificed first, the amortization fund next, except in the event of liquidation, and
the debenture element last. But with a little wangling the
amortization funds may be attacked before the equity
element in profit entirely disappears. The fall in the sum
available for profit and depreciation, determined as it is
by the relations of marginal to average prime cost and
marginal revenue to price, cannot be held up by any mere
sense that it is proper to maintain certain amortization
funds; be entrepreneurs as conscientious as they may,
what is not there cannot be paid into a fund; nothing
they can do can maintain those funds after a certain

point. For this reason there is some chance that a point may be reached, well above zero output, at which the necessary replacements and improvements of plant still profitable will exceed the greatest amount that can be got for the amortization funds, and that this excess will be sufficient to absorb what will be voluntarily saved at that level of output and income. This is the bottom.

It is to be hoped, indeed, that firms will not be too conscientious and will squeeze the amortization funds rather than dividends. For the more they do that, the less severe will the recession be. This is a good example of the vice of over-conscientiousness. It is now a commonplace that the borrowing of the Unemployment Insurance Fund in Great Britain in the years 1929–31 was a blessing in disguise, and that the measures taken to balance it in 1931 were economically mistaken. Conservatism with regard to habits of life is also to be welcomed; in the slump those do well by the community who spend above their income. The greater amplitude of recent fluctuations is probably due precisely to the fact that in the richer world there is a greater proportion of expenditure which can easily be cut down. Where needs are urgent and limited to primal appetites, men will prefer to live on their capital rather than to leave them unsatisfied. Living on capital maintains the volume of output because, by reducing the net propensity to save, it increases the volume of output consistent with any given level of net investment. The coexistence of conscientiousness with comparative initial affluence is the most favourable condition for a really large slump.

Once the bottom is reached, revival is likely to come, for the mere passage of time increases the amount of replacements required to maintain a given level of output. This increase involves a rise of net investment. This gives scope for the three dynamic determinants to ordain a period of steady or cumulative advance.

V. *The Inevitability of the Cycle*

The essence of the theory enunciated is that the cycle results from the joint operation of the Relation and the Multiplier. To bring this out, let us suppose a condition of steady advance. Every batch of hostages to fortune (net investment) is precisely justified by the result, and on the basis of this experience the advance is maintained. For this to happen the dynamic determinants must be operating in the way already described. Now let us do our best to suppose that they will continue to do so. What must we suppose?

It is probable that the first determinant will in any event be restrictive, that people will choose to save a rising proportion of a rising income. Their rate of saving might indeed be doctored by state interference, but to suppose that would be to introduce new data outside the scope of a study of how our system actually works. These will be considered in another chapter. But we need not despair on this account, since the restrictive influence of the first determinant may be offset.

The second determinant, the shift to profit, depends on the behaviour of costs and on the behaviour of the elasticity of demand. If the advance is not too great, the growth of population—but this is a factor which will shortly cease in the modern world—may stave off any tendency to Diminishing Returns owing to personnel. But the unpleasant side of that proposition is that it really supposes a rather high permanent level of unemployment. The growing inelasticity of demand is a more menacing factor, especially in a world becoming quite wealthy, and it may be sufficiently strong to cause a shift to profit in spite of all else.

It has generally been assumed since the onset of the industrial revolution that technological inventions are on balance 'labour saving'. It is not necessary, however, that this should always be the case. Certain conspicuous inventions, such as those of motor transport and wireless communication, appear to be of the opposite character. Investigation of present technological tendencies from this point of view is urgently needed. I am not qualified to make any pronouncement.

Attention may, however, be drawn to the modern tendency towards the more rapid obsolescence of machinery which should have some influence in making production *less* 'capitalistic'. This is obscured by the fact that the charge for capital goods, compounded, as it is, of interest and depreciation, is likely to be raised. Such a rise is quite consistent with the proportion which the interest charge bears to the value of the product falling, i.e. with the productive process coming to be *less* capitalistic.

On the side of durable consumption goods it seems not improbable that there is a tendency in certain departments against durability, for instance, if we consider the proportion of income devoted to housing, or the durability of furniture, clothes, motor-cars, &c. This tendency may not be unconnected with the general advance of income. As wealth increases, the desires satisfied by each increment are less narrowly determined by physiological needs, and the domain of fashion grows. In order to be in fashion it is necessary not to be too lastingly wedded to a particular commodity. As the scope of fashion-makers becomes wider (embraces a larger portion of the community's expenditure) the incentive to increase the pace of change grows. As goods become less durable, and their pattern also, the productive appliances required to produce them tend to be less durable. In so far as this happens the productive process is likely to become less capitalistic.

These considerations are not conclusive. They merely suggest scepticism with regard to the view that in the normal course of progress the proportion of capital goods to the income flow would, with a constant rate of interest, tend to rise.

On the other hand, the rate of interest may fall, and, if

it does so, this will exert an expansive force. The notion, however, that the rate of interest can be *made* to fall by the right amount to offset all restrictive forces is, in my view, entirely untenable; but I must reserve that topic for the next chapter. The third determinant is the most likely of the three to work in an expansive sense. If it exactly overcomes whatever restrictive force the other two may have, a steady advance may be maintained.

But it may not be maintained. We cannot rely on the three determinants to maintain it. It would be a blessed coincidence if they did. And here is the crux of the matter. If there is any drop in the rate of advance, a recession must occur. At that point the Relation dominates the scene. A decline in the rate of advance involves a recession of investment. But then, in accordance with the Multiplier, consumption must recede. Recession, once started, unless some big countervailing force appears in the midst of it, implies recession to 'the bottom'.

If the advance of net investment could increase or decrease by small amounts in company with general activity, the fact that the dynamic determinants were not likely precisely to offset each other at all times would be a matter of small concern. The trouble is that, when any decline of net investment sets in, a recession to the bottom is entailed and we have to begin the climb all over again from there; an ordered change from one rate of net investment to a lower one is impossible without this interlude. This is why, unless some reform can be devised altering the operation of the Relation and the Multiplier, we may confidently expect recessions to recur.

One must not exaggerate. A temporary downward fluctuation of net investment need not lead to a full recession. In the first place, such a fluctuation on the side of other capital goods may be offset by an opposite fluctuation of stocks (cf. pp. 72–4). Secondly, the existence of outstanding orders gives a breathing space during which the recession is held within fairly narrow limits, when some countervailing force may come into operation and save the situation. The United States probably experienced such breathing spaces in 1924, 1927, and again between July and December 1929. In 1924 the time was hardly ripe for a full recession; in 1927 it was averted, but not in 1929. The position was then complicated by the stock exchange situation, which will be discussed hereafter.[1]

A full recession involves, broadly speaking, the wiping out of net investment in the sense defined above. This accounts for the magnitude of recent recessions; net investment in the modern affluent world is so much higher than it used to be. It is probably a mistake to attach too much importance to the exuberances and follies of the boom. It does not appear that the level of activity at the bottom is very closely related to the level at the top of the boom. The problem rather is—how low must activity sink for net saving after deduction of losses (which include published losses and drafts upon hidden reserves) to be reduced to a level not very much above zero.

The view that future recessions are inevitable may be reinforced by this consideration. Could not the advance, it might be urged, be so restrained that it never reached a velocity which could not subsequently be kept up? Such a cautious advance could clearly not be greater than that warranted by the normal increase of population and the normal increase in efficiency through inventions and improvements within the period. Even so great an advance would be rash, since no given rate of improvement can be guaranteed to last (and in the modern world the advance of population is rapidly falling). Yet to accept such a solution would be to decree that there should never at all be any improvement in the unemployment situation (except such as can be secured by the use of surplus capital capacity);[2] if there is to be an improvement there,

[1] Cp. pp. 207–16.
[2] Reasons were given, on p. 57, why in the early stage of revival the slack of unemployed men and women is likely greatly to exceed the slack of capital capacity.

the increase must be such as to keep pace with new population and new inventions and also to take into work some of the existing unemployed. The present advance in England is already far above normal (1936). If the starting-point is one of large unemployment we must either acquiesce in that as a permanent feature or allow a rate of advance in output that cannot be permanently maintained. It is undesirable that people should acquiesce in large unemployment and highly improbable that they would take stern measures to ensure its continuance. It is therefore highly probable that a situation will recur in which the operation of the Relation and the Multiplier will once again produce a full recession.

Note on Saving

Use has been made in the text of an assumption, which is widely current in economic writings, that people tend to save a larger proportion of a large income. It would probably be difficult to give a rigorous justification of this assumption on *a priori* grounds. The following is a very brief summary of some general considerations.

Saving may be classified according to the motives which prompt it. The three principal motives are (i) to provide a capital sum available for future contingencies when abnormally high expenditure or defective earning-power is anticipated (ill health, old age, the education of children, &c.), (ii) to create or increase a regular income from property, and (iii) to acquire prestige and power by the possession of a large capital.

(i) The extent to which provision is made for contingent future needs should, prima facie, be roughly proportional to the extent to which current needs are met. Contingencies might, for instance, be actuarially estimated as the equivalent of a ten-year gap in earning-power. Saving should then be sufficient to bring income in the gap years up to net income in the earning years. This would involve an amount of saving proportional to income. It is not probable, however, that this generalization is true for low levels of income. The needs ordinarily catered for by this kind of saving, e.g. education of children, may not be as high on the preference list as certain primary necessities of life. Body and soul must be kept together, or the future contingencies will never arise. Nor, when present needs have a strong physiological basis, can people be relied on to make a nice rational balance between the advantage of present and future goods. Animal appetite is biased in favour of the present; adequate provision for the future presupposes that the appetites are sufficiently well satisfied for the motives arising out of prudence to have fair play. These arguments suggest that a lower proportion of low incomes will be saved.

(ii) Under this category general considerations vouchsafe a less clear answer.[1] If an individual is not biased in favour of the present, he should save so much that his net income (after saving is deducted) rises at such a rate that its marginal utility falls at a rate equal to the current rate of interest. One pound can always be transferred from this year to next with the addition of the current rate of interest.[2] If the marginal utility of unsaved income next year falls below the marginal utility of this year's income by an amount equal to the current rate of interest, nothing is to be gained (or lost) by such a transfer; therefore the optimum saving for the individual is that which makes the marginal utility of his income fall at that rate.

The proportion of income saved under this head depends on the rate at which the utility of income decreases per given fraction of income added. About this it does not seem possible to say much *a priori*. If the rate is constant for all levels of income a constant proportion of income will be saved. Thus, suppose the rate of interest to be 5 per cent.; and suppose that a 4 per cent. change in income per annum causes a 5 per cent. change in the marginal utility of income, e.g. that the marginal utility of £500 p.a. is equal to $\frac{105}{100}$ times the marginal utility of £500 × $\frac{104}{100}$ p.a. (= £520). It will be

---

[1] The classical exposition of the theory of this subject is given by F. P. Ramsey, *Economic Journal*, December 1928.

[2] This statement may appear to be in conflict with Mr. Keynes's Liquidity Preference theory of the interest rate. But it is not so really. The rate, according to his theory, must satisfy the marginal buyer of fixed interest-bearing securities who is just induced to hold them instead of money. We need not suppose that the representative saver is on the margin. The process of 'transferring £1 from this year to next with the addition of the current rate of interest' must not be regarded as that of purchasing a fixed interest-bearing security this year and selling it cum interest next, but of saving £1 more this year on which interest is earned in the next and saving £1 less in the next. The representative saver may be thought of as receiving interest as a consumer's surplus, owing to his comparative indifference as to liquidity.

proper, if the rate of interest is 5 per cent., to save so much that the unsaved part of income rises from £500 to £520. The fraction $\frac{104}{100}$ represents the amount by which spendable income has to rise in order to fall 5 per cent. in marginal utility. If the marginal utility of £1,000 p.a. is equal to $\frac{105}{100}$ times the marginal utility of £1,000 × $\frac{104}{100}$ p.a. (= £1,040), i.e. if the governing fraction, $\frac{104}{100}$, is the same for £1,000 p.a. as for £500 p.a., it will be proper to save so much that spendable income rises from £1,000 to £1,040; thus the proportion of his income which a man ought to save is the same in both cases.

Unhappily it is not possible to say *a priori* how the rate at which the utility of income decreases, as a given fraction of income is added, varies according to the size of income. If it is smaller, the greater the income, a larger proportion of a higher income will be saved. This analysis does not enable us to solve the problem set, but only indicates what would have to be known for the problem to be solved. Its result is thus negative.

(iii) The third motive for saving is as a means of acquiring additional prestige and power by larger capital accumulation. It is no longer a case of balancing the marginal utility of expenditure this year and next, but of balancing the marginal utility of expenditure in either against the marginal utility of the power and prestige due to additional capital. It may be doubted whether in the case of additions to capital made for this purpose the law of diminishing utility is not over-ridden by the law of increasing returns. Take the case of prestige. A capital of £4 millions may well be thought to carry not less but more than twice the prestige of a capital of £2 millions. The reason for this is that its possessor is esteemed not in proportion to the utility which he may derive from it, but in proportion to the skill required to obtain it. It may be objected that prestige can also be gained by lavish expenditure, so that the desire for prestige would pull in both directions, and it would be a matter of temperament which kind of glory the rich man preferred. But, if he adopts the method of display, he runs into the law of diminishing reaction to stimuli; whereas, if he saves, his glory becomes annually greater. As regards power, it is also not unlikely that the law of increasing returns will operate, £4 millions giving more than twice the power of £2 millions. Putting these things together it is possible that the returns in utility to large accumulations do not diminish. Since these have to be set against the diminishing utility of expenditure, a larger proportion of increasingly large incomes are likely to be saved. The incomes must be large enough for savings from them to make a substantial difference to power and prestige and for the marginal utility of expenditure to be sufficiently low to allow the power and prestige motives to compete.

The balance of these considerations appears to justify the assumption of the text.

Mention should be made of company reserve accumulation, now so large a proportion of total saving. This part of income is deflected to the saving stream not by individuals balancing the marginal utilities of present and prospective income, but by the policy of companies.

Bodies using public money for capital purposes are apt to have sinking fund provisions by which the capital is completely written off, and semi-public concerns to have stiff reserve requirements. The growth of public and semi-public trading is thus probably inclined to deflect a larger proportion of the income stream to saving.

CHAPTER III

INTEREST, MONEY, AND THE FOREIGN BALANCE

I. *The Rate of Interest*

THE most essential part of my theory has already been presented, yet the rate of interest and monetary policy, usually deemed matters of central importance, have so far only received passing references. This is no accident, but fairly represents the balance of my opinions. It must be recognized, however, that these factors do play a part, although, I submit, a subordinate one. If I incline in what follows to belittle their influence, this is designed rather as a corrective to prevalent views than as intending to deny that they are of substantial importance.

It is sometimes held or suggested that the rate of interest might, but for frictions or malpractices, be expected to behave in such a way as to correct the tendency to fluctuation; or, more moderately, it is held that it might be made by a wise or correct policy to behave in such a way. I propose to ask (i) how it would have to behave if it were required to hold the advance of output steady, and (ii) why it does not so behave. For that it does not we know. The consideration of these two questions will incidentally suggest an answer to a third, namely, whether it could be made so to behave.

(i) There are three points in the cycle at which we may ask whether the rate of interest might not have a decisive influence towards maintaining steadiness, namely, (*a*) during the upward movement, (*b*) when the decline of orders for capital goods first begins, and (*c*) during the depression. It is convenient to consider (*b*) and (*c*) before (*a*).

Reference was made in the last chapter to a breathing space, in which the rate of new orders for capital goods has begun to decline, but the amount of new capital goods in the course of construction, owing to outstanding orders, is not yet seriously affected. Such small decline as there is may be partly offset by the involuntary accumulation of stocks (cf. pp. 72–4).[1] This is the period immediately after the three dynamic determinants have decreed a slowing down in the rate of advance, and therefore a recession. The third dynamic determinant is the amount of capital per unit of output intended to be used in the productive process by the design of the capital goods most recently maturing. A highly 'capitalistic' design is a force tending to make for expansion. This design depends (i) on present technique, (ii) on the relation between the price-level of capital goods to that of consumable goods, and (iii) on the current rate of interest. The last of these affects both decisions as to the cheapest possible productive method in the circumstances and also the decisions of consumers in what proportion to divide their money between consumable goods having more and less capital embodied in them. (The batch of capital goods most recently maturing includes, of course, consumers' capital goods such as houses.)

If the joint action of the three determinants has recently decreed a slowing down of advance, a distinct fall in the rate of interest might produce a change in the situation. It would tend to make productive methods more highly 'capitalistic' and to deflect consumers' money towards the purchase of capital (durable) goods. New orders would flow in, giving effect to this. When the goods matured from these orders, the expansive power of the third determinant would be reinforced, and it might once again overcome the restrictive power of the other two. After a period of wavering the advance of production would assume its upward course, until the stimulus afforded by the lower rate was exhausted or the restrictive power of the other determinants became more severe.

[1] This is to be distinguished from the growth in the stocks of non-capitalist output (p. 99), which reaches the maximum at a later stage.

The suggestion should be noticed that the fall in the interest rate must be 'distinct', or, to speak more precisely, appreciable. One may like to think of the rate of interest falling steadily in the course of time. But if this is a long time, the fall per annum in the rate can hardly be greater than a small fraction of 1 per cent. A small fraction of 1 per cent. is not appreciable and is not likely to have *any* effect on the technique of production or the choice of consumers. Ordering capital goods entails giving hostages to fortune; there is necessarily a wide margin of uncertainty. I suggest that unless the safe rate of interest is thought to have fallen by at least, say, ½ per cent., the change is likely to have no effect. In making his calculations, the entrepreneur takes pencil and paper and writes down, say, 4 per cent., or, say, 3½ per cent. Nicer distinctions are not likely to be regarded as worth considering in view of the wide margin of uncertainty.

It might be objected that, in the course of a gradual decline of the rate, its effectiveness might operate through a larger number of entrepreneurs coming successively to interpret the existing rate as 3½ per cent. rather than as 4 per cent. This is a valid point. On the strength of it, it is possible to argue that, if the rate of interest has already been falling, an acceleration involving a fall within a short period of less than ½ per cent. might have a substantial effect. On the other hand, if, during the boom, the rate of interest has not been falling at all, then it is clear that the fall required to produce an effect upon the capitalist character of production must be appreciable.

Since we are considering the possibility of producing general steadiness and not merely that of avoiding a big recession after a particular 'evil day', it is necessary to ask whether the maintenance of advance by a reduction in the interest rate is not merely leading up to a more acute problem on some future 'evil day'. This depends on why the influence of the first two determinants is becoming more restrictive. If the first determinant, the tendency to save an increasing proportion of income, is responsible, it is possible that this tendency, being slow, steady, and secular, might continue to be offset by a steady downward secular trend of the interest rate. If the second determinant (shift to profit) is responsible, we must consider whether this is mainly due to the diminishing elasticity of demand or diminishing returns. The former is also likely, in the absence of the latter, to be steady and secular. But the latter is likely to become more acute if the advance is drawing on weaker and weaker human material. And the diminishing elasticity of demand is likely to become more acute also if the shift to profit due to the other cause is big. The matter also depends on the other circumstance affecting the value of the third determinant, namely, the state of current invention. If Professor Schumpeter's point is right, that inventions come irregularly, the situation is likely to be less tractable. Thus the possibility of an appropriate behaviour of the interest rate tiding over the immediate problem, without setting up a more acute problem later, depends on the circumstances. To this point we shall return very shortly.

Once the breathing space is past and consumption begins to decline, it is not likely that any behaviour of the interest rates can prevent, though a sufficient fall may mitigate, a large depression. For once the production of consumption goods begins to fall, net investment is reduced to the excess of the value of replacements over that of amortization funds. The low rate of interest may ensure that plant when replaced is made more 'capitalistic'. But the level of net investment, when depending entirely on replacements, is likely to be much lower, whatever the rate of interest, than it is when some advance is going forward. A low rate of interest, though it may somewhat raise the level of the bottom, cannot prevent a recession to the bottom once the breathing space is past.

This suggests that the reduction of interest rates, if it is to be effective in averting a severe depression, must be timely. Mr. Hawtrey has reached the same conclusion for somewhat different reasons.

It remains to consider how the rate might behave in the advance so as to produce steadiness. Here it is clearly a question of asking whether steadiness might be ensured if the rate rose more than it actually does. Taking up the point concerning the operation of diminishing returns in ultimately making the second determinant invincible, it might be argued that, if only the advance was held down to the rate at which diminishing returns did not operate, all would be well. At a certain crucial stage in the advance the interest rate might be kept higher than it has been wont to be, and later, as the increased propensity to save and the diminishing elasticity of demand tended to overcome the third determinant, it might be gently dropped.

But this brings us back to the crux already mentioned in the last chapter. If any given rate of advance is to be maintained in perpetuity, it must be limited to the rate of growth of population and efficiency. This means that any excess of the slack of unemployment over the slack of redundant capital capacity not obsolete can never be taken up. (An exception would be if in the early period of revival the size of the working population were increasing slowly and later much more rapidly. This case, having been mentioned, need not be considered further.) Such a policy for the boom would involve perpetuating the depression at a level not far from its worst. And even this policy, while it would *set the scene* for maintaining steadiness by a manipulation of the interest rate sufficiently clever to offset the action of the other determinants, would by no means *guarantee* the system from a relapse into still greater depression. And if this happened, the bottom would probably be lower than if prosperity had been allowed to return, since the volume of replacements would be lower. On the other hand, once allow the advance to be such as to take in part of the slack and it becomes certain that, if this rate is maintained, diminishing returns will supervene, and ultimately supervene with sufficient acuteness to check the rate of advance whatever happens to the rate of interest. And this involves a full depression.

Only if we were in the happy position of having a starting-point in which employment was fairly full and in which, none the less, the preceding period had not been one of advance greater than that of the secular trend, could we hope to maintain full employment and to avoid a major depression by very clever manipulation of the rate of interest. Though this is a highly improbable initial position, it is worth considering somewhat more carefully what behaviour of the rate of interest would in that case be consistent with a continuance of steady advance in various circumstances.

Since the rate of advance is conceived as no greater than that allowed by the secular trend, we may exclude Diminishing Returns as a restrictive influence. The remaining restrictive influences are (i) the tendency to save a larger proportion of a larger income, and (ii) the diminishing elasticity of demand. The importance of these is a matter of legitimate doubt. Whatever their importance, they are the influences to be overcome. They may be overcome if the productive process is getting more capitalistic. The conjoint operation of these three forces in justifying or terminating any given rate of steady advance has already been described in the last chapter. If inventions are of a highly capital-using kind, the rate of interest may even be required to rise. It must be noted that even if (i) and (ii) operated steadily through time, variations in the rate of interest would probably be required, since the operation of new inventions cannot be relied on to be steady. In practice the rate of interest would have to be moved, always supposing it to be susceptible to management, in accordance with the most recent experience. The rate of interest has been considered, so far, solely in its operation upon the value of the third determinant. But it may also have some effect on the first; of this we know less. It may be that a fall in the rate of interest will cause people to save a smaller proportion of their income and so reduce the restrictive effect of the first determinant. In this case the fall in the rate of interest would assist advance for two reasons, first because it makes the productive process more capitalistic, and secondly because it reduces the propensity to save.

There is a familiar ring about this last sentence. The reader may be reminded of the proposition derived from the traditional statement of the laws of supply and demand, that a fall in the rate of interest will at once stimulate the demand and restrict the supply of capital. And no doubt there is some connexion between that proposition and the statement of the text. But he will have read in vain if he supposes that there is more than a very distant cousinship between the static principles, enshrined in the traditional statement, which, being static, are essentially unadapted to performing the work required of them, and the principles governing the operation of the dynamic determinants in an advancing society.

If a steady advance is to be maintained, the rate of interest must so move as to provide a force which, when operating conjointly with the forces exerted by the propensity to save, the elasticity of demand for goods, and inventions, causes the three dynamic determinants to justify a continuance of the advance.

We ought, perhaps, to revert to the Law of Diminishing Returns. This was kept out of the picture in the foregoing paragraphs, since the advance, to be steady, had to be conceived to be in conformity with the long-period trend, and that eliminated the Law of Diminishing Returns from human material, since it might be supposed that a constant proportion of 'duds' in the community are kept out of employment. But what of Diminishing Returns from natural resources (the classical law)? It will be remembered that we got this out of the way by supposing the land to be mainly looked after by non-capitalist producers, in the narrow sense of that word, whose reaction in boom and slump is governed by entirely different principles. It might be suggested that this is a cowardly procedure and not allowable in a definitive statement of our solution, and that, anyhow, some natural resources, such as minerals, are extracted in a fully capitalist manner. This may be granted. The Law of Diminishing Returns, if relevantly operative, is a restrictive force requiring to be taken account of for the proper manipulation of the rate of interest. Its existence should be borne in mind. None the less, for convenience in what follows, since the distinction between an advance consistent with the secular trend and an advance of greater or less rapidity is of primary importance, and the operation of Diminishing Returns from human material is the chief feature which distinguishes the latter from the former, we shall use the term Diminishing Returns as applying to human material only.

In order to confirm ourselves in our grasp of the canons governing the behaviour of interest consistent with the idyllic condition of steady advance, we may ask how they are related to the canon proposed by Wicksell, namely, that the rate of interest should be consistent with the maintenance of a constant price-level. The behaviour of prices in the steady advance depends on (i) the behaviour of rates of reward to prime factors, (ii) the behaviour of the marginal efficiency of those factors, and (iii) the behaviour of the elasticity of demand (the three static determinants). The marginal efficiency of prime factors is likely to increase in any event, owing to improvements and also owing to an increase of capital equipment per head, if the rate of advance is great enough to secure that. This requires falling prices. The diminishing elasticity of demand, if it operates, requires rising prices. As to which of these forces is likely to be stronger opinions may differ. Nothing can be said *a priori*. A rise of rewards to factors, *ceteris paribus*, entails a rising price-level. If the combined operation of these forces requires the price-level either to rise or to fall in a steady advance, then, if the interest policy is designed to secure a constant price-level, it will be inconsistent with steady advance. But if steadiness of advance is not achieved, a full recession is inevitable; and in that event no interest policy can maintain a constant price-level. (Other possible methods of maintaining the price-level in depression will be considered in Chapter IV.) From this it seems to follow that the Wicksellian objective is unattainable, unless the static and dynamic determinants have certain particular values.

It has also been proposed that prices should fall in proportion to the increase of output per head or to the increase of total output. It seems likely that either of these conditions would push the rate of advance below the potential secular rate and so entail growing unemployment, and it is possible that they would inhibit advance altogether. We may make the supposition most favourable to the proposal, albeit one not likely to be realized in practice, that money rates of payment to prime factors do not rise. We may dismiss as freakish the supposition that marginal costs might fall in relation to average prime costs in a steady advance (economies of large scale would have the opposite effect).[1] We shall examine each proposal in turn.

(*a*) A fall of prices in proportion to the increase of output per head would in these circumstances allow of an advance in accordance with long-period potentialities, provided that there was no tendency for the elasticity of demand to diminish. But this, I submit, is unlikely. It is only probable if the advance were no greater than the increase of population, so that output per head did not rise at all (and then there would be no fall of prices!). If the diminishing elasticity of demand is accepted as a principle, then the advance by this criterion would have to be confined to that due to growth in numbers. But if improvements were occurring *de facto*, the advance would actually take the form of more output per man with grow-

[1] *Vide* p. 80, *supra*.

ing unemployment. And so even with this restricted rate of advance diminishing elasticity would probably come into operation (though the greater elasticity of demand of those out of work might to some extent offset this). With diminishing elasticity in operation it does not appear that any advance is possible. The static determinants would hold the system in equilibrium at a given level of output. Stability would be achieved at the cost of stationariness.

(b) The more deflationary proposal, that prices should fall in the same proportion as total output rises, might hold the level of output stationary, even if the law of diminishing elasticity were *not* in operation. Advance would only be possible even on that supposition if it did not entail an increase in total output greater than that of the output per man (increase of efficiency). In fact an increase of employment would in any event be impossible. The rigidly restrictive effect of these proposals would, of course, be relaxed if money rates of reward to factors of production fell.

It is time to return to reality. We are not likely to find ourselves in a condition of satisfactory employment with the immediately antecedent rate of advance no greater than that consistent with the long-period trend. Moreover, it must be remembered that even if we did, any serious mistake in the interest policy would bring about a full depression, and, having seen a glimpse of the promised world, we should be as far off from it again as ever.

(ii) The conclusions of the foregoing section being so largely negative, it seems that we can quickly dismiss the question initially proposed for this one, namely, why does not the rate of interest so behave as to secure a steady advance? Since it appeared that in real conditions no imaginable behaviour was likely to secure that result, we need not be surprised that its actual behaviour does not. None the less there are a number of matters regarding the actual behaviour of the rate of interest which it may be well to consider here.

What determines the rate of interest? Mr. Keynes has recently treated this subject with a princely profusion of reasoning. His contentions may be classified into their negative and positive parts. The negative part consists of arguments to the effect that there is no established theory regarding the determination of the rate worthy of the name. The two-dimensional static analysis of supply and demand treats of a demand price and a supply price *ceteris paribus*. But these other things include in this case the level of income and the rate of its prospective advance. In considering the demand and supply of a consumable commodity it may be legitimate to treat these things as constant. But in the case of saving, since it necessarily entails changes in them, such treatment is illegitimate. An increased propensity to save may be accompanied by a fall in the rate of interest; but it may not; it may equally well be accompanied by a decline of income; if this happens the demand for saving will at once be affected. Only if the level of activity and income is taken as otherwise determined does the traditional treatment of the rate of interest make sense.

Mr. Keynes's positive part consists of an original theory of the determination of the rate. He holds that it depends on a liquidity preference schedule and the quantity of money. Mr. Keynes's theory is neither inconsistent with nor necessary to what I have to say. To accept or reject it would involve lengthy discussion irrelevant to the essentials propounded in this volume. This means that I do not propound any positive theory of the rate of interest.

But some negative points of no little importance may be made. We know *de facto* that the rate of interest does not behave in such a way as to secure steady advance, for steady advance is not achieved. But we also know that the rate of interest behaves broadly in such a way as to promote steady advance; for it tends to rise in the boom, thus imposing a restrictive force, and it tends to fall in the slump, thus stimulating expansion. The rate of interest does not act as a de-stabilizer; quite the contrary. It follows that if we required of it that it should so behave as to decrease fluctuation, *ceteris paribus*, we should require it to fluctuate more and not less than it does. It might possibly be made to do so.

There are, however, strong forces, which it would be foolish to overlook, limiting its fluctuation. They might be partly overcome by manipulation, but they could not be wholly overcome. A distinction must be drawn between long and short rates. The latter are more amenable to control by the banking system.

The long rate of interest is of its very nature influenced by long-term considerations. The present rate is largely governed by what the rate is expected to be in future. Now the future, it is true, is shrouded in obscurity. But this does not mean that it is without influence. Suppose for the moment that the future is foreseeable and that it is known that at a given, not too far distant, point in the future, say in five years, the rate of interest will be 3 per cent. The present rate will not fall as low as $2\frac{1}{2}$ per cent., for if it did the prospective yield of a fixed interest security in the next five years would be less than zero. If it rose above 3 per cent., the prospective yield would rise far more.

What has the future in store? There are various possible rates of secular advance, and with each of these one determinate behaviour of the interest rate is alone consistent. It is not known what the rate of advance will be nor what the behaviour of interest necessarily associated with it is. If those things were known, it would be impossible for the present rate to diverge much from the rate foreseen as consistent with the secular trend. It would be impossible, therefore, for the present rate to behave in such a way as to do much to steady the advance. Our ignorance allows some flexibility in the long-term interest rates. But even ignorant people are apt to have a view, and that view influences their activity in pricing long-dated stocks here and now. They are not likely, therefore, to accommodate their pricing activities to the criteria of those who wish the rate of interest to fluctuate consistently with a steady advance.

If people had a true view, the rate of interest would not fluctuate in the convenient manner required. In fact they have views which lie on either side of the truth; but there is no reason why they should always lie on the side necessary to produce the fluctuation required for a steady advance.

Why the long-term rate is as accommodating as it is may perhaps be explained by Mr. Keynes's theory. In the slump liquidity preference recedes owing to the diminished calls of active business more than the quantity of money, while in the boom the reverse happens. This suggests that open market operations by the banking system may exert some influence over the long-term rate of interest; it must not be inferred that the influence can be extended to any amount desired.

The short-term rate is more volatile. It is probable, however, that this has far less effect on the level of net investment and activity. It is not likely to have a great effect either on methods of production or on consumers' choice. It affects the cost of carrying stocks. But the volume of these is influenced far more by the rate of turnover and the prospective movement of prices. And it must be remembered that the price of any particular commodity is likely to be subject to much larger possibilities of variation than the general price-level.

It is sometimes said that the rate of interest diverges from the natural level in boom and slump. If natural is defined as that consistent with steady advance, the proposition is clearly true. But there is *suggestio falsi* in the word natural. The natural level for the long-term rate may rather be regarded as that level at which, if dealers could foresee the future, it would stand. Of course, if they could foresee the future, the present rate would be different and therefore the future also. If this foresight were possible, we might well expect the rate of interest to be lower in the boom and higher in the slump than it actually is. For in the boom people are in fact optimistic and take too rosy a view; they think that present conditions are likely to continue. And in the slump they are too sceptical about the possibility of conditions materially changing for the better.

Take the circumstances most favourable for the steadying influence of the interest rate, namely, when employment is fairly good and none the less the immediately antecedent rate of advance has not been abnormally high, and when people are convinced that the steady rate of advance will be maintained. Suppose that in fact the varying incidence of inventions necessitates some such behaviour of the interest rate, to preserve the steady advance, as the following: in the first three years 4 per cent., in the next three 3 per cent., in the next three $3\frac{1}{2}$ per cent., in the next three $2\frac{1}{2}$ per cent., in the next three 2 per cent., in the next three $3\frac{1}{2}$ per cent. It need not be supposed that the transition from one level to another has to be sudden and abrupt; transitions may be supposed to be smoothed out. None the less, consideration of the yield of long-dated stocks makes it clear that these fluctuations are not likely to occur. The yields on 4 per cent. stock in the successive periods between the mid-points of the triennia would stand approximately as follows: 15 per cent., −3 per cent., 18 per cent., $15\frac{1}{2}$ per cent., −26 per cent. The long-term rate of interest is governed by the prices at which dealers in long-dated securities are willing to exchange them. It is very unlikely that in a steadily advancing society they would change their valuation in such a way as to cause this large variation of yield. It is unlikely that the variations in the interest rate required for steadiness would be secured. But the penalty for not securing them would be a full depression in the second and fourth triennia. If it be objected that the changes in the rates which I have supposed in my example are greater than would probably be needed, I can only urge that smaller changes are not likely to have an appreciable effect at all. Whatever the validity there may be in the argument that a persistent small rate of change in the rate, operating for a long time in one direction, takes effect through different batches of entrepreneurs successively taking note of it and treating it as an appreciable change, it does not apply if the changes are up and down.

It appears to follow that in conditions of steady advance we cannot expect spontaneous movements in the rate of interest sufficiently marked to secure it. It is quite true that we have recently had a fall in long-term rates, such that, if foreseen, the prospective yields of long-dated securities at their previous valuation would have been extremely high. But then we have been through the harrowing experiences of a great depression, which entailed a complete revision of opinion about prospects on the part of many people. We cannot expect that in the calm atmosphere of an advance, successfully maintained, long-term rates of interest would be continually popping up and down in the way required.

Mr. Keynes builds high hopes on the clever manipulation of the long-term rate by banking policy. In view of our profound ignorance about the future it is possible that long-term rates might be seriously influenced by banking operations carried on à l'outrance. To be sceptical about this is not to be sceptical about his theory of the determination of long-term rates. It only entails the view that his liquidity preference schedule is in certain circumstances extremely elastic.

Banking policy can push the present level of long-term rates below that which dealers expect to obtain at a future date by sufficiently reducing present short-term rates. When the banking system has reduced short-term rates to a nominal level it has exerted all the power it can by this method. It can only secure a still further fall in the long-term rate if it can persuade dealers to reduce their estimate of the long-term rate that is likely to obtain in future. But how can it do this? Not assuredly by threatening to bring about a further fall, for it cannot bring that about unless the dealers are persuaded, and it cannot use the threat that it will do so, therefore, as a means of persuading them. If it had sufficient information at its disposal it might demonstrate that a steady advance with full activity could only be achieved by a further fall in the long-term rate. But this demonstration would be irrelevant unless it could also persuade the dealers that such a steady advance was, in fact, destined to occur. Now that the static theory of interest has been laid on the shelf, it cannot represent that there are any 'natural forces' which will secure such an advance. Nor can the banking system promise to secure this advance by its own manipulation of the interest rate, for the possibility of that manipulation depends on the dealers being convinced, and, once again, it cannot use as an argument to convince them the inevitable advent of a state of affairs, which is only inevitable if they are convinced, and is highly unlikely to happen if they are not. Thus it seems improbable that banking policy, however inspired and well informed, could secure a sufficient fluctuation in long-term interest rates to ensure a steady advance.

II. *Money*

The set of ideas to which the doctrines of this essay are most repugnant are those connected with the Quantity Theory of Money. This is a curious upshot. For many years monetary doctrine, squarely based on observable phenomena, simple, and appealing to our most elementary logical faculties, requiring no postulate of laws of unmeasurable utility or unverifiable preference schedules, has been thought to be the securest part of economic theory. Yet now all seems changed.

It must not be supposed that any challenge is offered to the validity of the Quantity Equation, on which Quantity Theory doctrines are based. In the developed theory there has always been a weak spot, namely, the velocity of circulation. The Quantity of Money is an observable phenomenon, and the proximate causes at least, which govern it, may be specified—the volume of bank lending, &c. Velocity is also observable, but the causes which govern it are less easy to distinguish. What theory of velocity, it might be asked, have you to advance which will be consistent with this theory of the cycle? To which it might well be answered that perhaps there is no further and separate theory, that this doctrine of trade fluctuation is itself the theory of velocity. Those forces which have been enumerated govern the volume of output and the level of prices; these in turn cause the velocity of circulation to be what it is. Or rather, they cause the quantity of money multiplied by its velocity of circulation (MV) to be what it is. And velocity is the resultant of banking policy, which determines the quantity of money, and of the forces enumerated, including any effect that banking policy may have, for instance via the rate of interest, on the forces enumerated. On this view it is the variations in velocity that enable money to behave as a lubricant to the system and to allow it to follow its chosen course. In particular they enable money to act as the arch-destabilizer, overcoming the stabilizing forces of the static determinants and allowing the level of output to move up and down as the dynamic determinants prescribe.

But suppose, it might be objected, that velocity refused to behave in this accommodating way. We might be asked to trace out the consequences of supposing velocity to be constant. Then it is quite true that the dynamic determinants could not have the effects here claimed for them. The system would not behave as it does. What would happen? I cannot trace out the consequences of that hypothesis. It appears to be of the kind which may properly be called illegitimate. We know that velocity is subject to variation. The logical consequences of supposing the opposite are so radical that it would be necessary to construct a complete model of an economic system different from anything we know. It would be like an exercise in pure geometry, and harmless so long as it was kept quite pure and did not claim to represent what would happen in the real world if all was as we know it but for this constant velocity. On the other hand, if any one claims that he has a theory about what does govern velocity, conformable with experience and based on sound reasonings, which is inconsistent with the behaviour of velocity that I postulate, let him bring it forward so that his reasonings may be pitted against mine.

An attempt will be made to deal with certain leading difficulties that may be felt with a view both to overcoming mental resistance and to exploring the possibilities of monetary policy.

Consider the case of a depression. As output and prices recede, then, unless the quantity of money is reduced in proportion, which it often is not, monetary balances will become abnormally large in relation to the work which they have to do. Why do people tolerate this? Why do they not push them out into use, and, in so doing, restore the level of prices and output? One hears of idle balances. Why do they lie idle? The conviction that, if people have money they will use it, is responsible for the most dogmatic pronouncements of quantity theorists.

Of course, we know that in fact they do not use it. But what is the rational explanation? An attempt will be made to give one. A warning, too, must be given. We are about to enter that treacherous and dangerous region where time-lags are met with at every turn. Man, used to a straightforward one-dimensional time, finds living difficult when he has to step and re-step between districts where the clocks are behaving differently, and with no foreknowledge as to how the clocks are behaving anywhere. It is a prerequisite of obtaining substantial knowledge here that we should know much more about who holds the idle balances in different phases of the cycle.

Hypothesis is no substitute for investigation. The suggestions which follow are of an interim and tentative nature. In this respect their status is entirely different from the propositions about the cycle which derive their cogency from the nature of the relation, the multiplier, and the determinants.

A beginning may be made by considering an hypothesis advanced by Mr. D. H. Robertson, that the amount that people spend in any period is related not to what they earn in that period, but to what they earn in the preceding period.[1] This seems a sensible view and it is worth while to explore the consequences. Mr. Robertson is so convinced of its importance that he has suggested a definition of saving of his own, by which the amount of saving in any period is defined as the difference between the spending in that period and the income of the previous period. This definition will not be used in these pages. To reject the definition as inconvenient does not involve denying that people may tend to behave in the way that Mr. Robertson suggests. It is more convenient for us to retain a single definition of saving throughout this essay; Mr. Robertson's definition would have rendered the statement of the fundamental principles of the second chapter much more cumbersome.

The period that Mr. Robertson has in mind is some kind of circulation period; its value is clearly very different for different sections of the community. For instance, the wage-earner may be expected to spend his wages fairly quickly, and for him the period may not be more than a week or two. On the other hand, the profit-earner's period is something much greater. The earning accruing to him

---

[1] See *Economic Journal*, September 1933, Mr. D. H. Robertson, 'Saving and Hoarding', p. 399. It should be observed that Mr. Robertson does not postulate that people invariably or even regularly behave in the way described. But he regards such a behaviour as a norm, in the sense that he would define any deficiency of their disbursements in one period compared with their income of the preceding period as hoarding and any excess as dishoarding.

as shareholder takes a long time, it may be sometimes as much as eighteen months, to filter through into his pocket. The lag in the fall (or rise) of expenditure behind that of income would thus be different for different classes. Mr. Robertson's hypothesis probably represents the maximum lag likely.

If we suppose there is *no* lag, the money withdrawn from circulation in a recession of income stays in the hands of those who held it beforehand. It will probably be treated by them as a monetary reserve no longer needed and used on the first opportunity to purchase more remunerative assets. The consequences of the attempts by holders of money to swap it for revenue-yielding assets will be traced after we have examined Mr. Robertson's hypothesis. As there is in fact likely to be some lag, its consequences ought to be considered. Mr. Robertson's hypothesis is taken as representing the most extreme view.

In a condition of steady advance it has no significance; indeed, it is doubtful whether a lag is an appropriate concept in this connexion. If income rises steadily and a constant proportion is saved, expenditure will rise contemporaneously with income; it may be possible to identify the pennies spent on the nth day with those received on the mth; such identification is of no economic interest. If a steadily rising proportion of income is saved the rise of expenditure will still from day to day bear a constant ratio to the rise of income.

But in the event of a transition the lag becomes important. If the transition is upward an abnormally high proportion of income is saved in the period of the lag, and if the transition is downward an abnormally low proportion. Thus when a revival of replacements comes, the normal effect of the multiplier on general activity will not be felt. Indeed, at first there will be no repercussion on general activity. The system will continue to 'bump along the bottom' for a little longer than it would otherwise do. This point has, indeed, already been noticed in an embryonic form; we saw that until earners in the replacement industry began to spend their earnings, the whole of the saving required for the new net investment was found by them. If we also take into account the considerable lag between the profit-receipts of a firm and their expenditure by its shareholders, it appears that the multiplier may not exert its normal force for a considerable period; or, to put it otherwise—and more strictly—during the period of the lag the value of the multiplier is abnormally low.

Conversely, when the boom reaches its peak the lag would postpone recession. The propensity to save being abnormally depressed during the lag, the value of the multiplier becomes abnormally high, and the recession of general activity is not so great in relation to the recession of investment as it would be if the value of the multiplier were normal.

When we think of this point in relation to wage-earners it does not appear to be of great importance, their lag period being so short. When we think of it in relation to profit-earners, it merges almost imperceptibly into the general point made in connexion with the shift to and from profit. For that shift also gains its significance, precisely because the expenditure of profit-earners has a looser relation to their income, so that variations of income are to an abnormally large extent taken out in a variation of savings. The effect of Mr. Robertson's point is that this abnormality is larger in the period immediately following a shift than subsequently. This point may be added to the others enumerated on p. 99 as a reason for the path of the slump not being so precipitous as the naked argument based on the properties of the Relation and the Multiplier indicated. As the profit-earners gradually adapt their expenditure to their new income position, the value of the multiplier returns towards normal and, without any further fall of investment, activity continues to recede. And investment may also continue to fall if the continued recession of activity further reduces the volume of replacements.

Mr. Robertson's hypothesis has enabled us to approach, but it has not taken us right up to, the problem of what happens to the surplus money. If his view is correct, that money will not be left with the general public except in so far as they fail to invest their regular savings. At the end of any circulation period they will hold money equal to the income of that period. If income, having been £10 per period, recedes to £8, then at the end of the first £8 period they will only hold £8. For they held £10 at the beginning of that period, and during it, while only earning £8, they disbursed £10, in accordance with Mr. Robertson's hypothesis that people normally disburse their income of the previous period. Thus at the end of the period they only hold £8. If every one behaves in this way, the general public disposes of the surplus money in the first circulation period of a recession and reduces its cash holding to what is appropriate to its reduced level of income.

If the whole community does this, what becomes of the money? It might almost seem at the first blush that we could prove with the aid of Mr. Robertson's formula that, unless people take to hoarding, a recession is impossible! If only people keep on spending the income of the previous period, will they not keep on earning it? The total money-value of goods produced could never change! We should be back in that state of society which monetary theorists, if they were as pure as they sometimes pretend to be, *ought* to believe natural and necessary, in which prices only rise when output falls and only fall when output rises.[1]

But this conclusion does not really follow from accepting Mr. Robertson's formula. Still ruling out the possible hoarding of saving by the general public in monetary form, we must consider the condition of firms. In so far as their profit is concerned we treat that as the income of the shareholders. But what about the capital assets?

[1] Cf. p. 40.

When orders for net investment first decline, income accruing from current consumption does not decline in the first circulation period, since the public is spending an amount related to its income of the preceding period. But in the second circulation period something does happen to income from the sale of consumable goods. For some producers of net investment were thrown out of work in the first circulation period, and having no income in that period or, anyhow, a reduced one, they cannot, according to Mr. Robertson's formula, maintain their consumption in the second. Where does the money that thus goes out of circulation get to? It remains in the hands of the firms whose activity is affected by the decline of net investment. In the period prior to the decline they received money from sales as usual. But they at least do not expend their receipts of the previous period in the first circulation period of the decline, for, lacking orders, they cannot distribute it all to their employees. It remains in their hands. They cannot legitimately distribute it as dividends, for it is not a profit. It is a capital asset; in the first circulation period of the recession their assets consisting of goods in process are lower and the difference is made up in cash. Since, having insufficient orders, they cannot distribute this cash in wages and salaries, as previously, they may wish to use it to buy securities. This point takes us on to different terrain and will be considered shortly.

This explanation may be generalized so as to solve our problem. When firms reduce activity their pay-bills fall; in the first period of the fall receipts accrue in respect of the activity of the previous period; if the receipts exceed the pay-bill of the previous period, that excess is profit; they will exceed the pay-bill of the present period by still more, since the present pay-bill is lower and receipts proportional to the pay-bill of the previous period are still coming in; but that additional excess is not profit. The circulating capital of a firm may be thought of as a block of money which is exchanged for goods which are then sold for money at a profit; the circulating capital then resumes its money form once more. If activity recedes, in the first period of recession it is impossible to push out the whole of this money in exchange for further productive services. Thus there will be a surplus cash holding, which represents part of the firm's capital. Part of the money of the community will have been shifted from being circulating medium proper to being a capital asset.

It must be understood that I am not laying down that in a slump money is absorbed in this way. The argument is merely an exercise on Mr. Robertson's theme that the expenditure of the general public is related to their income of the previous period and that they refuse to let the surplus money stay with them. It has been shown that it does not follow from this that all the money goes on circulating. On the contrary, when the determinants decree a recession the residue is trapped into being part of the capital assets of firms. Of course, they will then try to exchange it for some more remunerative capital asset. That is the second part of the story.

It may be well, however, to prolong the first part a little further. In the full account given in the last chapter the beginning of the recession involved certain changes in the rate of advance before a decline actually began. The value of the second differentials moved first and set up a change in the value of the first. These niceties may be neglected here. We may suppose that in the first circulation period of the recession there is an actual decline of net investment, and therefore of total income. Expenditure on consumption, being related to the income of the previous period, does not fall. In the second period it will fall. What income do the entrepreneurs responsible for providing consumption goods pay out in the first period? Here we are up against the difficulty that the circulating period of physical circulating capital may be different from the circulation period of money, and innumerable variations may be examined by making different hypotheses.

To simplify matters I suppose these two circulation periods to be the same. The next difficulty concerns the lag of entrepreneurs in diagnosing the situation correctly. Let us take the two extremes, (i) that the entrepreneurs responsible for consumable goods diagnose the situation in advance, and (ii) that they only learn by experience.

On the first supposition the entrepreneurs are aware that the demand for consumption goods will be lower in the second circulation period. Therefore they should reduce output in the first. Therefore the demand in the second circulation period will be lower still, since, if they reduce output and income in the first period, the expenditure in the second circulation period will be *pro tanto* lower. The situation being a nasty one, they will be prepared for lower prices. To what extent they meet the situation by reducing output and to what extent by allowing a reduction of prices in the second circulation period will depend on the value of the three static determinants. They must arrange matters so that the prospective marginal revenue in the second period is equal to marginal cost in the first. To what extent this allows a fall of prices depends on the stabilizing force of the three static determinants, viz. the fall in rewards to factors and in real marginal cost owing to the reduction of output in the first period together with the increased elasticity of demand owing to diminished expenditure in the second. Of course, all these things cannot be worked out precisely. Entrepreneurs will gain experience as the depression proceeds.

While the distribution of adversity between a restriction of output and a fall in prices is governed by the static determinants, the amount of adversity will depend on the value of the multiplier. The matter is complicated by the fact that the profit circulation period is much longer than that of the prime factors. Try to get rid of this complication. Suppose all income were prime factor income. Entrepreneurs in the consumption trades would then have to reduce their outlay, and therefore total income, in the first circulation period sufficiently to reduce total saving in the second by the amount of the reduction of net investment in the first circulation period. Only if they did this would they find their costs in the first circulation period covered in the second. Or suppose that there was no greater lag of profit than of other income. The profit earned in the first circulation period might be calculated as the excess of prospective receipts in the second (which would depend on what was done in the first) over prime costs in the first. To be right in the second they must so reduce output that the consequent decrease of savings by prime factors plus the concurrent decrease of savings from profit, reduced as calculated, was equal to the reduction of net investment in the first period. To get rid of the special profit lag we suppose the profits realizable in the second period to be distributed, like prime factor rewards, in the first. As income accruing to the consumption trades from the expenditure of earners in the investment trades is down, to get right the entrepreneurs must see that the proportion of earnings in the consumption trades that is spent is correspondingly raised, or that the excess of costs, including profit, over expenditure by earners in the consumption trades is correspondingly reduced. This is done by a reduction in the absolute amount of activity and so of earnings in those trades. In the real world there is a large profit lag. This means that in each of the early circulation periods (measured by the prime factors' period of circulation) expenditure is higher, according to Mr. Robertson's formula, than it would otherwise be. The recession in the consumption trades is delayed accordingly, as has been explained already.

In the first circulation period the receipts in the consuming trades are maintained, but their outlay is reduced. This excess of receipts over outlay does not represent profit and cannot be distributed as dividends. The reduced outlay implies a reduction in the volume of physical circulating capital. The surplus money in hand must be reckoned as part of the firm's capital. Thus the withdrawal of money from circulation, so surprising to the quantity theorists, has a natural explanation.

The firms with these money balances may reduce their indebtedness to the banks. In that case the Quantity of Money will recede in proportion to the fall of turnover. But the firms which find themselves with money in hand vice circulating capital may not be the same as the firms indebted to banks, or, anyhow, the money in the hands of various firms may not be proportional to their indebtedness. In this case bank loans will not be reduced in proportion and velocity of circulation will drop. We have still to see what happens when the firms with surplus money try to exchange it for external remunerative capital assets. The smallness of the reduction of bank indebtedness, which is so often found to occur in the early stages of the slump, is, so far as it goes, evidence against Mr. Robertson's hypothesis that people tend to spend the income of the last circulation period. Wage-earners may do so; their period is short. But by the time profits, the time-lag in the circulation of which is big, come into their owners' hands, the profit-earners know perfectly well that things have got worse and that their future income is in jeopardy; and at this stage they will surely have begun to reduce expenditure accordingly. If that is so, the profit earned in the good time and paid out later does not come back to the firms, and this may partly account for their inability to reduce their indebtedness to the banks.

If the entrepreneurs in the consumption trades do not anticipate the bad turn of events in the first circulation period, their receipts in the second will be greater, but marginal revenue will fall below marginal cost. They will certainly take action in the second period. It cannot be said *a priori* whether the amount by which they should reduce outlay in the second period, if they are wise, is greater or less than the amount by which their receipts fall. If the latter is the case they will entrap no money. The implication of this is that the money entrapped by the investment industries is sufficient to reduce the money in active circulation by the required amount. It might be thought that it would take some time before the consumption trades learn by experience to anticipate events. But this does not appear to be what actually happens, since stocks of consumers' finished goods are reduced fairly rapidly in the slump.

It may be well to set out in 'real' terms what happens when expenditure is protracted in the way alleged, after earning has fallen, and when firms are thereby enabled to supplement their capital by a cash balance. In the normal course the community generally sells its services to firms and takes their products in exchange. In the case supposed when the sale of services (= earning of income) is reduced, the consumers say—'Well, go on selling us goods a little longer and take our surplus money in exchange; we do not want it.' And this very process keeps activity alive a little longer in the consumers' trades; but only for so long as this surplus money is being surrendered. For the segments of activity, which are in the process of dying, can only be kept going so long as there is an extra source of demand for them coming from this surplus money. They cannot keep alive by taking in their own washing. The process of keeping them alive constitutes a transfer of the ownership of money from the general public to the firms. This money may be gold, or it may be banking liabilities. If the latter, it consists in the last analysis of a part ownership of the assets of firms to which the banks have lent money (including the government). Thus this surrender transfers to the firms the part ownership of what are mainly their own assets. In so far as the right firms receive the money, they will regain control of their own assets by repayment of bank indebtedness.

This final kick of the consumers leaves firms more solvent. We may have here another aspect of the general tendency of growing affluence to make the depression more troublesome. The poor spend what money they have and are likely therefore to behave in a Robertsonian way. The rich have spare money in hand in any case, and begin to curtail their lavish expenditure as soon as the newspaper reports of the Stock Exchange tell them that they are poorer men—long before the profits cease to flow in.

The going in these last paragraphs has not been easy. They will have been useful, even if in no other way, if they have demonstrated to the reader how troublesome this country of time-lags is. Alternative hypotheses might easily have been framed. Their very multiplicity suggests that we cannot hope much of the *a priori* method in this field. Luckily the main part of our theory of the cycle is not beset with such difficulties.

We must now proceed to the second part of the story. What happens when the holders of the surplus cash try to exchange it for more remunerative assets? It is important to emphasize that we are here concerned with the exchange of one capital asset for another. The money has moved over from active trading circulation and acquired the status of a capital asset. Nothing that happens to the capital market in consequence can have the *direct* effect of sending it back into circulation. It may happen that an individual with some idle money at the bank, which has come there in consequence of certain capital transactions, may say—'Well, why should not I just spend it?' This will indeed have a momentarily stimulating effect on production. But the effect is bound to be temporary and the money is bound to revert again to its capital status in some other hands, unless and until the dynamic determinants decree another upward advance. So long as they impose a barrier to expansion, no presence of idle money can influence the situation.

The presence of idle money which its holders are trying to exchange for other forms of assets may, however, have an *indirect* effect on activity. The volume of new capital goods coming into existence is equal to the volume of current saving. Thus the titles to these new capital goods may be acquired directly by the savers without any shift in the prices of these titles, or indirectly, if they purchase old capital assets from those who use the sales proceeds to purchase other old capital assets from those who use the sales proceeds, &c., &c., to purchase the new capital assets. There are no further new remunerative capital assets for the firms to purchase who acquire money vice circulating capital in the slump. Thus the demand for remunerative capital assets by holders of money rises above the supply. This may cause a rise in the prices of remunerative capital assets.

It must be observed, however, that whatever the prices of remunerative capital assets, some one must hold the extra idle money. The prices of remunerative capital assets must rise so far that there are sufficient people who think it worth while to hold money as a capital asset rather than purchase remunerative capital assets at the inflated prices, for all the idle money to be so held. (Mr. Keynes's theory of liquidity preference.)

Capital assets other than money may be divided into two sorts, (i) titles to which a fixed rate of interest is attached, and (ii) titles to the residual share of the yield of capital goods. Now with regard to the second class it must be observed that although the demand for them has increased more than the supply, their prices may not (and indeed in the slump quite clearly do not) rise. This is because the adverse turn reduces their prospective yield and reduces the present value of that capitalized at any given rate of interest. The increased demand for capital assets may reduce the rate of interest, but, even so, there is no reason to suppose that the reduction of prospective yield will not more than outweigh the higher rate of capitalization. Thus, despite the quantity theory, the prices of consumable goods and capital goods (class ii) may well fall together.

The prices of fixed interest securities, on the other hand, may be expected to rise unless the adverse turn has undermined confidence that the interest will in fact be paid. This involves a drop in the rate of interest, increases the expansive force of the third dynamic determinant, and so is favourable to an increase of activity.

It is important to guard against certain misconceptions. We have at last found something the price of which may be expected to rise in a slump. It must not be thought that the quantity theory in its plenary sense can be rehabilitated, that the prices of fixed interest securities may be expected to rise so much as to offset falls elsewhere and leave the general price-level proportionate to the quantity of money. The notion that the general price-level may be expected to vary in the same proportion as the quantity of money is only appropriate when the whole stock of money is passing along the income stream, when holders of money do not care how many units of it they hold provided that they hold in money the power to purchase so many goods, e.g. to finance their purchases for a week or a month. In these circumstances the price-level will vary in the same proportion as the quantity of money; the elasticity of the demand for money will be equal to one.[1]

When part of the stock of money is used as a capital asset, these rules no longer hold. The rate of interest which induces people to hold fixed interest securities instead of money and vice versa depends on a variety of factors. The curve showing the preference for one compared with the other as a function of the rate of interest may have an elasticity far greater than one. Mr. Keynes has treated this point so skilfully and exhaustively that it is unnecessary for me to labour it. I will only reinforce his arguments by laying stress on the importance of the prospective rate of interest. We are dealing with a phase of the trade cycle which, as such, is not likely to last. There may be a definite view about the future of the rate of

[1] For the measure of elasticity see footnote on p. 86.

interest. A very small fall of the present rate below that wipes out the prospective yield of fixed interest assets and so destroys all advantage of holding them rather than money. It is for this reason that open market operations, which increase the quantity of money available to be held as a capital asset, may not have a very great effect in certain phases of the cycle in reducing the long-term rate of interest.

Still less reason is there for supposing that the fall in the rate of interest, which is likely to occur in a slump for the foregoing reason, may be expected to restimulate the system to its previous level of activity. That would only be so on the palpably false assumption that people were absolutely unwilling to hold money as a capital asset (that is, if the elasticity of demand for it as such were equal to zero) and that they would bid the price of securities up and up until the consequential fall in the rate of interest and the consequent stimulus to trade took the idle money off again into active circulation.

The view is sometimes suggested or implied that in a slump the rate of interest ought to fall sufficiently to re-stimulate activity, and, if it does not, this is due to some lag, or friction, or interference, or mismanagement. If the foregoing argument is right, there is no substance in this view.

It may be noticed that whereas on the Robertsonian hypothesis regarding the spending habits of people the firms or entrepreneurs (in their capacity of producers, not of income-receivers) are the first to acquire idle balances in the slump, they do not necessarily retain them. In regard to the problem where the idle balances finally go, the firms, the new savers, and the former holders of other capital assets are all on the same footing, pitting their own judge-ment against that of the market. Some may think that the market is undervaluing certain capital assets; they will buy those assets. Others may think that the market is overvaluing all capital assets or those specially suited to their requirements; they will hold money. The new savers may be advised by their brokers to wait a little before investing their surplus. Those who have just sold assets to cut a loss or consolidate a gain while it is still possible may look around in vain for another form of investment which they judge wise or suited to their purposes. Thus there will be a thorough reshuffling of the idle balances.

It is hoped that the foregoing paragraphs will have done something to overcome the mental resistance of those who, on the basis of the quantity theory, are unwilling to believe that the price-level can so easily fall in consequence of the action of the static and dynamic determinants.

Something may next be said about the power of monetary policy to determine the trend of events. The influence of the banking policy is greatest on the short-term rate of interest; it has already been argued that this is not a factor of major importance in governing the level of activity. The banks may endeavour to influence the long-term rate by purchasing securities in the open market. By this operation the banks and the general public exchange remunerative assets and banking obligations. The quantity of the former in the hands of the public is decreased and the latter increased. This should raise the value of the former and *pro tanto* stimulate activity. But it cannot be argued *a priori* that, if the banks go far enough with this policy in a depression, the consequent fall in the rate of interest will be sufficient to check it; it is likely, however, somewhat to raise the level of the bottom. Moreover, if the rate of interest is already standing at a low level in relation to prospects, great open market operations may be unable to depress it substantially. The public may be willing to hold large extra quantities of money rather than mark up securities very much higher.

Some confusion appears to have arisen with regard to the power of the banks to control the amount of investment. It has been implied that if the banks increase their loans investment must increase, not merely in so far as a fall of interest occurs and so makes more capitalistic

methods profitable, but as a direct and mechanical consequence of the increase of loans. It is represented that, if
the banks make additional loans, the loans must be used by
some one, and the use of the loans is additional investment.

I believe this notion to be entirely erroneous and to have
arisen through some confusion arising out of a past controversy concerning the power of the banks to increase
the quantity of money in circulation by increasing their
loans. If the community is in the habit of using the IOU's
of the banks as money, it seems clear that the banks have
this power. The late Professor Cannan, despite his usual
clear-headedness, refused to the end to admit this point.
But it seems irrefutable and is now, I believe, accepted by
all professional economists of standing.

But it is one thing to allow that the banks alter the
quantity of money by their loan operations. It is quite
another thing to allow that their loan operations produce
a direct variation in the quantity of investment in the community. I believe that much confusion has been caused
by the too-hasty assumption that the latter proposition is
entailed by the former. It is even possible that, if it had
been clearly pointed out that admitting the former did *not*
involve admitting the latter, Professor Cannan's reluc-
tance to admit the former might have been substantially
weakened.

As lenders the banks are hopelessly and irretrievably in
the position of middlemen. They can only lend what is
lent to them. The exception to this is if they pay out what
they lend in gold. Otherwise, when the banks lend, the
public must lend back an equal amount to the banks on
deposit. The amount that the banks lend to industry is
precisely equal to the amount that the public lends to the
banks on deposit. The banks are mere conduit-pipes.
They have no power of making the saving available for use
in investment greater on any day than the amount that
people are choosing to save.

How, it might be objected, is this reconcilable with the

observed fact that, if the banks increase their open market purchases, they may cause a downward movement in the rate of interest? The matter may be explained quite simply. When the banks come into the open market to buy they say in effect: 'We are willing to hold a larger amount of the remunerative assets of the community of greater or less liquidity and to give in exchange our own obligations redeemable at sight.' Thus they enable the community to hold more of its savings in the form of quite liquid assets and less in a less liquid form. The banks may be said to underwrite the liquidity of part of the capital assets of the community. Thus the desires of a greater number who attach special importance to liquidity may be satisfied, and a smaller number, outside the banks themselves, are required to hold the more remunerative but less liquid assets. The marginal demand for liquidity on the part of those outside the banks, now that a greater volume of liquid assets is available, will be lower and the marginal demand for remunerativeness will be higher. This will tend to raise the price of remunerative assets and lower the rate of interest.

This effect may cause the determinants to alter the level of activity and investment. But there is no presumption whatever that the extra investment will be equal to the extra loans made by the banks. It may quite well be much greater or much less.

Objection to this doctrine might take another form. Surely, it might be argued, if a new opportunity for profitable investment occurs (the determinants justify an increase of investment) and the banks are there ready to lend the money, this willingness to lend may render the investment possible where it would have been impossible without their assistance. That is quite true. It is not proposed to deny that the banks perform a most important *technical* service in concentrating and canalizing the savings of the community. In the absence of banks it might be impossible for an advance to proceed, even with the goodwill of the determinants, owing to the technical difficulty of mobilizing the savings, which, in the event of the advance being undertaken, would be available. Thus it would be impossible to carry out the advance and the savings would never be realized. This may be granted. What is denied is that the banks can provide the means of investment when in the event of such investment there would, apart from the banks, *be* no savings available for the purpose.

III. *The Foreign Balance*

The argument so far has been concerned with a 'closed' system, not subject to the extraneous influence of a balance of payments with an outside world. It applies therefore to the world as a whole. Manifestations of the cycle have recently been world-wide; the depressions of 1920–2 and 1929–32 were so; recovery was proceeding at varying rates in all countries in the years 1925–9, and, despite the great variety of circumstances and policies in different countries, there was a remarkable synchronization, with but a few exceptions, in the recovery of 1933. Thus it appears by no means out of accord with the facts to regard the world as a single unit for these purposes.

None the less there are national differences. If each nation was entirely isolated from the rest, it is improbable that the observed synchronization would occur. It is important, therefore, to consider how the world phase of the cycle transmits its influence to each particular country. In the last analysis that influence can only operate through the commercial relations of the particular country with the outer world, of which its balance of payments represents a numerical summary. In a particular country the scene may be set for further advance; yet, if in the world as a whole the determinants decree a depression, that country may find itself drawn in by strongly adverse forces operating through its foreign balance. It is not improbable that Great Britain was in that position in the year 1930. It is desirable, therefore, to formulate the principles which relate the level of a country's total activity to its activity in dealings with foreigners.

The simplest way to approach this subject is by reverting to the conditions envisaged in Chapter I in which no capital accumulation is occurring. We may then develop the concept of another 'multiplier', call it the foreign trade multiplier. If the world level of prices and the state of foreign markets are given and the rates of reward to prime factors at home together with their degree of efficiency in producing goods at home are also given, then, assuming a fixed rate of foreign exchange, a determinate value of goods visible and invisible will be marketable abroad. There may also be a net income from foreign investment. These two together constitute the total of 'active' items in the balance of payments. The income constituted by them is expended. Part of it is expended on home-produced goods, part on foreign-produced goods. The former expenditure gives rise to further income, which is in its turn similarly divided, and so on. Total home activity will be such that total income is such that, given the propensity of consumers to purchase foreign-made goods, the value of those bought will be equal to the value of the active items. Thus the foreign payments balance. If people spend the whole of their incomes, foreign payments must balance. For income received from the sale of goods at home is equal to the expenditure on home-made goods, total income is equal to total expenditure, and, therefore, the residue of income, that accruing from abroad, must be equal to the residue of expenditure, that devoted to the purchase of foreign-made goods.

The level of activity is thus conceived to be related to the value of income from abroad by a multiplier, the value of which is determined by the propensity of people to spend on foreign goods. This concept of a foreign trade multiplier is precisely analogous to that of the multiplier developed in the last chapter, by which the level of total activity is related to the volume of current net investment by the propensity of people to save. Before considering the interrelation of these multipliers it will be well to examine the conditions of a non-accumulating society more fully.

First, consider the relation of the foreign multiplier to the static determinants. The fourth of these is the level of prices. In the first chapter the probable value of this was considered in relation to the quantity of money and its velocity. In the case of a country forming part of a world system and in trading relations with other countries, the prices obtainable for exportable goods and for goods subject to foreign competition in the home market are determined not by monetary conditions within the country, but by world conditions. Thus, so far as activity in making goods open to foreign competition is concerned (and this does not preclude the existence of tariffs and other trade barriers), the value of the fourth static determinant is governed by world conditions.

What of the level of prices of goods not subject to foreign competition? If the doctrine of the foreign multiplier is accepted, and, in the conditions stated it does not seem possible to gainsay it, the level of general activity may be deduced from the level of activity in producing goods open to foreign competition. This being so, the price-level of the non-competing goods must be such that, taking into account the values of the other three static determinants, this level of activity occurs. Here again money is seen to act as a mere lubricant. The doctrine here enunciated contains the germ of truth embodied in the theory of Purchasing Power Parity. There is no force tending to make the level of non-competing prices in a particular country equal to that in any other country. But there is a force connecting the level of domestic activity with the level of activity in the production of goods competing on the world market (the foreign trade multiplier). And there is only one domestic price-level consistent with this level of activity in the production of domestic goods. In this indirect way the price-level of non-competing goods is governed by world conditions.

Monetary manipulation within the country, given a fixed rate of foreign exchange, cannot alter this. The banks may increase the quantity of money by open market operations, but unless these have some effect on the active items in the foreign balance or on the propensity of people to purchase foreign goods they cannot alter the domestic price-level. The banks and the public will merely be induced by the open-market operations to exchange one form of capital asset for another.

Next suppose a shrinkage of world activity to supervene upon a given situation. A decline of the active items may be expected and a consequential general decline. The general decline of income need not be in proportion to the decline in the active items, since there may be a change in the foreign trade multiplier. The accommodating performance of the non-capitalist producers in 1929–31, together with the inelastic demand for their products *in toto*, considerably increased the multiplier in Great Britain and enabled her to proceed through the depression with a much smaller decline in her general activity than in her export items even before any protective measures were introduced.

Of the balance of payments during such a recession it is not possible to say anything in general. In the world as a whole money will move over from active circulation to capital account. About which countries will entrap the money it does not appear that anything can be said *a priori* at this stage. If the assumptions that people spend their whole income and that capital is maintained intact are taken strictly, the balances of payments should remain in equilibrium. The money will be entrapped in the country in which it is beforehand.

The foregoing account of the relation of the level of activity to foreign conditions involving the doctrine of a multiplier is similar in substance to one which I gave when attempting to expound the elementary theory of the balance of payments in simplified conditions in another volume.[1] I then proceeded to take capital movements into account, without going deeply into the relation between the propensity to save and the demand for capital goods. I assumed that the fundamental principles which would prevail in the simplified conditions would also do so in the more complicated case in which capital movements are taken into account; this treatment was in accordance with orthodox doctrine, but in the light of the earlier analysis of this essay it requires radical reconstruction.

It is necessary to examine the relation of the savings multiplier to the foreign trade multiplier. At first sight it might appear that there is a conflict of principle; but this is not really so. *Both* the active current items in the foreign balance *and* the volume of net investment at home serve as bases which if appropriately multiplied determine the level of total activity. And there are not two multipliers, but one. The multiplicand is the value of the active current items and the value of net investment at home taken together; and the multiplier depends on the proportion of income which people choose to spend *on home-made goods*. It is constituted by the ratio of their total income to their total income less what they spend on home-made goods. Thus if people spend two-thirds of their income on home-made goods and the value of the active current items and the value of current net investment at home may each be represented by the numeral 1, the income derived from the production of goods produced and consumed at home will be represented by the numeral 4 and total income by the numeral 6.

It is well at this point to recall attention to the relation between static and dynamic analysis. Static analysis proceeds by asking what rate of flow of goods per unit of time through the exchange process is such that, given tastes,

[1] *International Economics*, ch. vi, secs. 1-3.

&c., no party to the exchange feels disposed to alter his conduct. This analysis is appropriate to a society which does not accumulate; it is a perfectly proper instrument for dealing with the problems of international interchange in these conditions.

But, if accumulation is proceeding, income is growing. The volume of net investment and the rate of interest, that is, the current price which has to be paid for the means of current net investment, are both magnitudes which are essentially related to this process of growth. No static analysis can give a correct account of their determination; yet this is what the traditional analysis of value and distribution has sought to do. Mr. Keynes has perceived that there is something radically faulty in the traditional theory of interest; his perception is related to the objection here stated, since he partly bases his case on a criticism of the traditional presupposition of a constant level of income. But he does not formally set out the proper method of dynamic analysis.

This method should proceed by asking the following question. What is the rate of growth which, if maintained, will leave the parties content to continue behaving in a way consistent with it?

One is naturally reluctant to complicate the theory of foreign trade with dynamic considerations; for a complete theory may be set out that will be valid for static conditions; unlike the volume of investment, the magnitudes with which the theory of foreign trade is concerned do not of their essential nature involve growth. Yet one is driven to the view that in the real world the determination of the foreign trade magnitudes is dependent on dynamic forces; this is especially due to the operation of the multiplier.

It will be remembered that the condition required for a steady advance, before foreign trade was taken into account, was that the increment of expenditure due to the current increase of income, connected by the multiplier with the current increase of net investment, should give

full employment to the maturing capital goods. The ful-
filment of this depended on the operation of the three
dynamic determinants. In the new state of affairs it is still
true that the condition for a steady advance is that the
increase of production should give full employment to the
maturing capital goods. But this increase in the use made
of maturing capital goods is no longer solely due to (i) the
increase of expenditure on home-made goods, but also (ii)
to the increase of exports. Moreover, the former of these
increases can no longer be related solely by the savings
multiplier to (a) the increase of net investment *at home*, but
depends also on (b) the way in which an increment of
expenditure is divided between home-made and foreign-
made goods, and (c) on the increase of current active
items. For in the new conditions the multiplicand consists of net investment at home *plus* the current active
items.

The new situation may be met by the introduction of
two new dynamic determinants in addition to the three
which operate in a closed system, namely, (4) the ratio of
the increase of active current items to the increase of net
investment at home, and (5) the proportion of a rising
expenditure devoted to foreign-made goods.

If the values of the three domestic dynamic determinants are constant in a given condition of steady advance,
or if, while not constant, the changes in their values
exactly offset one another so that the steady advance continues, then, if the above-mentioned foreign dynamic
determinants retain a constant value, the steady advance
may be maintained. Or, a steady advance may be maintained if, while the resultant of the domestic dynamic
forces changes, the resultant of the foreign dynamic forces
changes in such a way as to offset this.

To explain, let us take as our starting-point a condition in
which all five determinants retain a constant value in a state
of advance. A constant proportion of income is saved, there
is no shift to profit, methods of production do not become

more or less capitalistic, active current items increase at the same rate as net investment at home, and a constant proportion of income is spent on foreign-made goods. To show that the last two conditions are appropriate for a steady advance, suppose the opposite. (i) Suppose that *ceteris paribus* (i.e. the values of the other *four* dynamic determinants remaining constant) active current items increase at a greater rate than net investment at home. Total income will increase at a greater rate. Expenditure on home-made goods will increase at a greater rate than capital goods are maturing. And so will exports.[1] But this will produce an acceleration of advance. Suppose that active current items increase at a slower rate than net investment. Total income will increase at a slower rate also. And so will exports. It will not be possible to make full use of maturing capital goods. (ii) Suppose again that *ceteris paribus* a smaller proportion of a rising income is spent on foreign-made goods. The rise in expenditure on home-made goods will exceed that for which the maturing capital goods were designed. Conversely, if a larger proportion of a rising income is spent on foreign-made goods, the rise in expenditure on home-made goods will be insufficient to give full employment to the maturing capital goods.

Of course, it is not necessary for a steady advance that all these values should remain constant as incomes rise. It is sufficient that the changes should be such as to offset one another. Thus if the domestic determinants are

[1] Strictly a further condition is required for steady advance, namely, that the increase of exports should be proportional to the increase of active items. An increase of exports and an increase of income from foreign investments operate somewhat differently upon the situation. For, whereas they both operate on total income, through the multiplier, and so on the domestic demand for home-made goods, an increase of exports also gives employment to maturing capital goods on its own account, while an increase of income from foreign investments does not. Thus if the five dynamic determinants were constant a rise in the proportion of active items due to exports would be a force making for expansion, and conversely.

set fair for recovery they may overcome the restrictive influence of a fall in the ratio of active current items to net investment. Similarly a world recovery entailing an increase of active items may allow recovery to take place at home in circumstances in which the domestic determinants by themselves would not permit it. Hence the tendency of recovery to spread.

Now although an increase of active items may not be necessary to the maintenance of an advance, a decline in a rate of increase of active items which has once been established may upset the apple-cart. For, if a steady advance has been maintained with the assistance of a given rise in active items, then, if that rise becomes less, the steady advance can no longer be maintained, unless by a blessed chance some favourable change occurs in the three domestic determinants. If no such change occurs the general advance of activity must slow down, but this spells a full depression. Thus a decline in the rate of increase of active items, if this is of appreciable importance, is likely to entail a full depression. Consequently, however much a particular country in a recovering world damps down its own increase of net investment at home, it is likely to be involved none the less in a recession to the bottom when a world slump comes.

Not much need be said about the fifth determinant. A rise in the proportion of expenditure devoted to foreign goods would be a restrictive force, and conversely. There may be some tendency for a rising proportion of an increasing income to be spent on services or on goods containing a high rent element owing to local fashions. This tendency, if operative, might give an additional lease of life to an expansion.

Expenditure on foreign-made goods should include the purchase of foreign-made raw materials required in the production of home-made goods. Imports of foreign-made raw materials required for the production of exports should be deducted from the active items and from exports. Imports of foreign-made capital equipment should be deducted from the total of net investment at home.[1]

It must now be quite clear how a depression of substantial importance occurring in the world is transmitted to those countries not yet ripe for it. However the domestic dynamic determinants are behaving, a depression in the outside world causing a deceleration in the increase of exports, *a fortiori* one putting an end to that increase or causing a decline, is likely to cause a full recession at home. For a slowing down or cessation in the increase in this important section of the multiplicand is likely to cause a slowing down in increase of total income. But this, in accordance with the Relation, causes a decline of net investment at home, and so of total income, and so a recession to the bottom.

When the bottom is reached the dynamic determinants may allow a revival without the assistance of an increase of exports.

So far the influence of foreign conditions on domestic activity has been considered without reference to the net balance of payments. It is by no means a condition of a steady advance that the net balance on current account should be zero; that is an unlikely eventuality. For it to be fulfilled the ratio of net investment at home to active items would have to be equal to the ratio of saving to the purchase of foreign-made goods. The flow of specie (and/or short-term claims) depends on the relation of the balance on current account to the amount which people choose to lend or borrow abroad. So far as the dynamic determinants are concerned, a steady advance does not imply that specie is not flowing.

If specie is flowing in there should be no obstacle on the

---

[1] The foregoing argument concerning 'net investment at home' is independent of whether that is financed by domestic or foreign capital. The international movement of capital is considered very briefly below in connexion with the balance of payments.

monetary side to a given steady advance; in so far as the inflow causes a fall in the rate of interest, it may be a force making for expansion through the operation of the third dynamic determinant. If specie is flowing out, the central bank may have to take special measures and check the rate of advance. This will precipitate a depression. There are thus two possible and quite distinct causes for a depression in a particular country, namely, (i) if the five dynamic determinants decree it, and (ii) if the banking system decrees it owing to an outflow of specie. The second cause is the less likely to operate the easier is foreign lending. For a country receiving extra specie is likely to wish to exchange it for interest-earning assets, and the only way it can do that is by investing abroad and so checking the flow from countries losing specie.

It is important to emphasize the distinction between these two ways in which the foreign balance may operate in an adverse sense. It is probably safe to assert that the American reverse of 1929, the *fons et origo* of world disaster, was due to the operation of the three domestic determinants. In Great Britain it is likely that the fourth dynamic determinant, the loss of active items, played a predominant part in the early stages. In Germany, on the other hand, the advance decreed by the domestic determinants in the years 1925–9 was such as to produce a passive balance on current account; in a prosperous world this was naturally and easily financed by borrowing. After the bad turn of events she was confronted with a problem additional to those presented by the operation of the dynamic determinants, the specifically monetary problem of a passive balance.

In analysing the relation between foreign transactions and internal activity, traditional theory has been inclined to place too much emphasis on the net balance of total payments. Thus foreign transactions have been represented as stimulating internal activity only if they were such as to entail an active balance, and conversely. I am indebted to Mr. S. D. Pollard for having pointed out to me very lucidly that this is a fundamentally mistaken view. An increase of exports may so stimulate internal activity as to entail a greater increase of imports; the consequential passive balance, so far from being a sign that the totality of foreign dealings are exerting a restrictive influence, may indicate precisely the opposite. Of course, in the long run a passive balance will, unless covered by movements of capital, have to be dealt with by the banking system. But a restrictive banking policy, intended to cope with a passive balance of payments, may be pursued over a considerable period and yet fail to counterweigh the expansive effect of foreign relations if active items are rising. A high interest rate is only one force among many operating through the dynamic determinants on the acceleration of production. In a boom, we have already seen, the rate of interest is likely to be comparatively high in any case.

The net balance of payments is observed to give more trouble in the slump than in the boom. There is no prima facie reason why items on current account should have a greater tendency to balance in the one than in the other period. But in a slump there is far less net investment. This, taken together with the lack of confidence that then prevails,—and in international investment confidence is especially requisite—may explain the observed phenomenon that the balance of payments gives more trouble in a slump. Discrepancies on current account are less easily and naturally covered by international lending.

A passive balance aggravates difficulties in a slump. Countries afflicted with it may meet the trouble in two ways, (i) by protectionist policy and (ii) by restrictive banking policy. The former aggravates troubles elsewhere, not only owing to the fact that countries hitherto exempt may develop a passive balance, but also—and this is probably more important—through the operation of the fourth dynamic determinant, i.e. by a reduction in the active items of other countries. This will have an adverse effect upon them even if, and indeed, the more so if, their active *balance* is not thereby reduced but increased. The restrictive banking policy is even more disastrous, since it lowers the bottom of the slump for the country concerned, and, probably, thereby for every one.

If a country does not maintain fixed rates of exchange the difficulties arising from a flow of specie are removed. But it is not likely that she will gain exemption from the effects of world changes operating through her active items. If a cessation of increase occurs she may indeed endeavour to restore it by exchange depreciation. But a rate of increase which depends on wresting a progressively larger share of world markets and diverting trade progressively further from the channels which it would otherwise follow is not likely to be long maintained. The gain from having a free exchange is substantial and important; but it should not be regarded as a panacea.

The dynamic analysis of a free exchange régime is not altogether easy, since one important part of the multiplicand, namely, the value of exports, becomes indeterminate.

Consider the early stage of recovery, when the domestic determinants decree some advance. If the advance occurs foreign purchases are likely to increase. If there is no increase in active items, the central bank may be compelled in gold standard conditions to exert a restrictive influence through the rate of discount, and hold up the recovery in the interests of the standard. If we now suppose that the gold standard is not in operation, and the rates of foreign exchange are allowed to move under the influence of supply and demand, the recovery may go forward. It should be noticed that the new condition allows of greater recovery than is accounted for by the mere removal of the restriction imposed by the necessity of maintaining an even balance of payments. This restriction might have been removed by supposing that it had been possible to cover any passive balance by borrowing.

The free foreign exchange does more than this. Not only will such recovery as the domestic determinants decree be allowed to go forward, but also the fall in the rate of exchange will have an *additional* stimulating effect. For it is likely to raise the level of one part of the multiplicand, exports, above the level at which it would otherwise have stood, and, unless the demand for imports is inelastic, it will raise the value of the multiplier, a larger proportion of income being spent on home-made goods. Thus any advance entailing a downward movement in the foreign exchange rate is likely to accelerate more rapidly than it would if the old par had been preserved and its tendency to generate an adverse balance had been met by foreign borrowing.

There is some temptation to proceed from this point and consider a state of advance in which the rate of exchange is steadily moving downwards. Such an investigation would take us too far from experience. There is something which arouses suspicion in the notion of a steadily falling rate of exchange, as in that of a steadily falling rate of interest, although this latter concept has been used by the most distinguished economists. And for the same reason. These continuous downward movements are apt to be anticipated, and therefore discounted, and so rendered discontinuous.

It may fairly be hoped that a free exchange will be used to prevent a steady advance ever having to be brought to a termination through an outflow of specie. Further, it may be hoped that in the more far distant days of international co-operation the exchanges may be systematically moved in one direction or another by joint agreement in accordance with long-period trends. It does not appear that analysis of the effects of a steady movement in the exchanges in a non-co-operative world subject to the trade cycle can be usefully carried farther in this context.

CHAPTER IV

THE QUESTION OF REMEDIES

I. *Remedy and Diagnosis*

REMEDY depends primarily but not entirely on diagnosis. In the first place the diagnosis must be accepted by a sufficient preponderance of recognized authorities. But in the economic field the application of remedies may involve the co-operation of a large number of persons outside the ranks of experts. These may be unwilling to acknowledge the authority of economists to prescribe; the existing state of economic studies gives some justification for such scepticism. The habit of mind engendered by their practical duties, and in general no doubt qualifying them well for the performance of these, may make them incapable of themselves understanding the diagnosis presented; or they may not be interested in the cure of the trade cycle. It may be expedient to urge a less efficient remedy if it is more likely to be widely acceptable. Thus he who seeks a remedy finds a host of psychological questions arrayed behind the scientific one of diagnosis.

It may be well to give a re-capitulation of the leading features of our diagnosis. The cycle is conceived to result inevitably from certain outstanding characteristics of our economic structure. This view may be contrasted with those which attribute it to exuberances and exaggerations, to bouts of unwarrantable optimism and imprudence, to mismanagement of some sort. According to the analysis here set out, the cycle would occur even if every one had perfect foresight and behaved with perfect good sense; and it may be expected to become more accentuated.

It does not follow that it is absolutely incurable within the general limits of our economic structure. It does follow that it is not likely to be cured by a more rigid observance of traditional maxims, or by an increase of sagacity on the part of enterpreneurs or bankers. Nor is it likely to be cured by the spread of better information, business forecasting, or discussion by the most enlightened business men and statesmen in their off hours. The disease goes too deep for that and cannot be tackled by the methods of the amateur. It is only likely to be cured when it is specifically recognized as such, and when the view is accepted that scientific method is necessary for its remedy. Expert bodies must be set up, backed by the authority and resources of government, to make investigations and give advice requiring the most prompt execution; the tiresome paraphernalia of research must be called into being. The problems of the trade cycle are as little likely to yield to half-time treatment as those of aerial warfare; and preparedness for speedy action is equally necessary. Initiative, with all its pains and ardours, in a new field of endeavour is required; the stubborn resistances of established habit must be overcome.

The cycle is here conceived to be necessarily connected with the process of capital accumulation. Previous writers on the subject, guided by the clue which the facts provide, have endeavoured to formulate theories connecting the cycle with this process. These have contributed many points of interest, but have missed the necessary links which make the theory here set out an intelligible and self-consistent whole.

That theory depends on the twofold nature of capital accumulation. On the one hand there are the decisions of those who order the construction of capital goods, having in mind that the uses to which they will be put in future are likely to yield a profit. On the other hand there are the decisions of those who decide to refrain from consuming a part of their incomes, in order to make provision for the future. These two sets of decisions are made by different people, but are necessarily mutually interdependent. Effect cannot be given to the former without the latter, nor to the latter without the former.

The capital goods cannot be constructed, unless the where-withal is surrendered by income receivers for this purpose. The view that bankers can conjure up the wherewithal *ex nihilo* has been shown to be fallacious. Nor can income receivers set aside funds for future use, unless new capital goods are concurrently created to the ownership of which they can acquire the titles. The alternative methods that suggest themselves, viz. the purchase of already existing capital goods or the loan of money to others for purposes of consumption, entail a corresponding amount of *dissaving* by other income receivers. Similarly, if they wish to hoard their savings in money, they can only increase their hoards to the extent to which the stock of gold (or silver) is itself growing, except at the expense of dis-hoarding some one else. (If the banks 'create' new money by their credit policy and the savers hold the new deposits so created, they are indirect holders of capital goods either new or disposed of to the banks by dis-savers.) The *net* saving of income receivers must be equal in value to the new capital goods concurrently being created.

Attention should be concentrated in turn on each of these sets of decisions. Of paramount importance for the former is the rate at which the whole level of activity and consumption of the community is advancing. New houses are required because there are more people to live in them or because the existing population, with a growing income, is able to afford more house-room. Additional manufacturing machinery is required because the turnover of manufactured goods is growing, that is, because consumption is growing. Let the growth cease and no additional machinery will be required. There will still be some work in the machine-making industries on account of replacements; but replacements are financed out of replacement funds; the production of replacement goods does not by itself enable any would-be saver to give effect to his wish to set aside some of his income for future use. Since replacements are of no avail, the only kind of capital construction which allows an individual to give effect to his desire to lay by, is the construction of additional capital goods. This construction will only be undertaken if there is expected to be a profitable use for the goods. This expectation depends primarily on the prospect of a growth in consumption.

Primarily, but not entirely. Inventions may occur making new capital installations profitable even in a society otherwise stationary. It is sufficient for our thesis that a considerable proportion of the construction of additional goods depends on the prospect of growth.

What of the second set of decisions? Here the determining factor is quite different; it is not the prospect of an increase of income but the absolute level of income at the moment. People do not set money aside because they expect their incomes to grow; on the contrary such an expectation would probably in most cases be a consideration on the other side. They save because their incomes are sufficiently large for them to satisfy urgent present needs and to set aside something to meet future contingencies. The amount of saving depends primarily not on the prospective rate of growth, but on the present size of income.

Here then we have two magnitudes, each of which represents the sum total of a large number of decisions made quite voluntarily by individuals (including companies, &c.) to suit their own particular interests. Yet these two magnitudes are really but one magnitude. For they are necessarily and ineluctably equal. It is the interaction of the two sets of motives which gives rise to the cycle.

The nature of this interaction may be most clearly apprehended by considering the critical point at which, either owing to a decline in the prospective rate of growth of consumption or to a fortuitous shrinkage in the stream of inventions requiring capital installation, the demand for additional capital goods goes down. If the amount of saving done by individuals depended on similar considerations, that too would be reduced. The two magnitudes, which are but one magnitude, might be expected to jog down together in harmony, and some advance, albeit a slower one, would be maintained. But the change in prospects which affects the demand for capital goods, does not affect savers in the same manner. For instance, if the increase of income slows down but the absolute magnitude of income does not fall, they will not choose to save any less.

Thus we are confronted with a situation in which the orders for capital goods are reduced, but savers are not disposed to save any less. When this happens those responsible for purveying consumable goods become faced with a falling market. For the purchasing power which savers keep out of the market for consumable goods is no longer fully made up by the expenditure on consumption of those engaged in making capital goods. On the first impact of this situation, stocks of consumable goods are likely to accumulate. In spite of intentions, the two magnitudes are kept equal, partly by the loss of income and consequential reduction of saving owing to the loss of profit on unsold goods, and partly by the fact that the value of new capital goods for which orders were given is supplemented by an increase, albeit unintended, of capital goods of a different sort, viz. stocks in hand. But this situation spells depression. For with stocks piling up, orders for consumable goods will be reduced and production and income will run down. This process of running down will continue till incomes are so reduced, that people do not choose to save from them more than is required for financing the now reduced level of capital construction appropriate to a slower rate of prospective advance. The prospective reduction in the rate of growth will thus have caused a slowing down all round.

But this is not the worst of the matter. Indeed, it is only the beginning. With the reduction of consumption, capital goods will become redundant, and for the time being *no* new capital goods will be needed to provide for a prospective advance of consumption. The first set-back in the capital goods industries was merely due to a slowing down of the prospective rate of advance. This led to a certain amount of depression all round. But now there is likely to be a second and far more severe set-back in the capital goods industries. For now no provision whatever is required for an immediate prospective advance of consumption. This sets up a further discrepancy between the intentions of those who give orders for capital goods and the intentions of savers, far greater than the original discrepancy. This by the same reasoning brings another much larger wave of trouble for the consumable goods industries. The process of income-reduction, which is trade depression, will go on, until incomes are so reduced, that what people choose to save from them is no more than that required to finance the construction of capital goods to meet demands for them other than those arising from prospective advance. This is depression indeed.

Thus the reduction in the demand for capital goods, whatever its cause, not only involves depression throughout all industries, but brings upon the capital goods industries, and again consequently upon the others, a far greater depression than could be directly accounted for by the original reduction of demand.

It need not be supposed that a large depression occurs on every occasion of a shrinkage in the demand for capital goods. In the foregoing chapters the existence of a 'breathing space' has been noticed, giving time for something new to turn up and save the situation. Furthermore, our economic structure being so complex and different countries being economically linked together, there is some probability of forces offsetting each other, a shrinkage in one place being offset by an increase elsewhere. None the less it would be too optimistic to hope that this will always happen.

The case for a recurrence of depressions being likely is immensely fortified, when we take into account the fact that they have happened in the past. For in a revival consumption grows at a rate that cannot possibly be maintained. At the outset the slack of human capacity available for work is greater than that of capital equipment, since the former has been maintained and grown at its normal rate during the slump, while the latter has not. After the revival has proceeded a short distance therefore, the demand for capital goods arising out of the (abnormally high) prospective increase of consumption stands at a level at which it cannot be maintained. The increase of consumption must slow down, once a considerable proportion of the unemployed is taken back into work. Consequently a point is bound to come at which the volume of orders for additional capital goods, which it appears profitable to give, is reduced, and this, in accordance with the foregoing reasoning, spells a major depression.

Standing in the way of a clear recognition of the relations set out above has been a fallacious theory regarding the rate of interest. It has been supposed that the two magnitudes, which are but one magnitude, would be brought to equality, without the cyclical disturbance arising, through suitable changes in the rate of interest; just as the supply of a commodity is brought into equality with the demand for it by appropriate changes in its price. The fallacy resides in a misuse of the assumption, 'other things being equal'. These 'other things' include the present level of income and the prospective rate of advance. Now it may be legitimate to assume that these factors can be regarded as fixed and given in the determination of the amount of a particular commodity to be produced and to concentrate attention upon the relation between its utility to the consumer and its cost of production giving effect to an 'equilibrium' price. A similar but, this time, illegitimate procedure in the case of saving would be to concentrate attention on the demand for capital due to technological causes and on the propensity of consumers to save out of income taken as given, and to suppose that the amount of saving is determined by a rate of interest which brings demand into equality with supply.

The fallacy consists in assigning sole potency to certain features in the situation, which are in fact often of subordinate importance only, and in treating as fixed, given, and pre-determined certain features, viz. the level of income and its prospective rate of advance, which are in fact not pre-determined but variables in the situation. Once this is recognized, it becomes apparent that the demand for saving may be brought into equality with the supply of it, not by variations in the rate of interest, but by variations in the level of income and its prospective rate of advance. It has been my main task to trace out how this happens.

In the course of this task, certain reflections have suggested themselves of wider significance for economic theory. In the formulation of the laws of demand and supply, as applied to a particular commodity, it has been necessary to make certain abstractions. It has been usual to suppose a certain given state of technology and a certain given set of desires on the part of consumers, and to ascertain what is the equilibrium price and the equilibrium amount of output of each commodity consistent with these circumstances. If a change in these circumstances occurs, then a new equilibrium will in due course be reached consistent with the new situation. This is static analysis.

Saving necessarily involves growth; for an increase in the amount of capital goods involves an increase of productive power. In order to determine an equilibrium volume of saving, it is necessary to take this factor of growth explicitly into account. It is no longer appropriate to ask—as in the case of a particular commodity—what amount of saving will be justified on the assumption that the surrounding circumstances remain the same within the period in which the equilibrium is established. For the saving itself entails a change of no little importance in the surrounding circumstances, viz. a growth of productive power. The question has to be asked—what amount of saving will prove justified, *taking into account the factor of growth* which the saving necessarily entails? Whenever saving is in question, the factor of growth must appear as an explicit term in the laws of supply and demand. The doctrine of the 'dynamic determinants' set out earlier, constitutes a tentative approach to this new branch of economics. But it is merely a rough sketch of what ought ultimately to be so elaborated, as to constitute the second main division of any treatise on economic principles. Fresh fields of thought await the pioneer.

The economic mind has recently had some awareness of these possibilities. But it has been distracted by considerations which are of great interest but irrelevant to this main theme. The static analysis has been felt to be insufficiently comprehensive, but, in order to break its bounds, writers have thought fit to lay emphasis on the importance of institutional arrangements, of frictions and of time-lags. Coming nearer to the heart of the problem, other writers have sought to make economics more dynamic by taking more fully into account the effects of anticipation on the static equilibrium. But even this approach does not give us what we want. The question is not simply—what effects will certain anticipations have on the present situation? Rather it is—what anticipations will have such results in the future as to justify those anticipations? And in answering this we have to take account of the fact that the world, in which the justification of those anticipations will be tested, will by reason of their having been entertained be different from the present world. The static analysis, even when taking account of the existence of anticipation, supposes the governing conditions to remain constant within the period in which equilibrium is established, and is therefore inadequate to deal with the rate of interest, of saving, or the size and growth of income.

Variations in the rate of interest appear to do something to make activity steadier than it would otherwise be, for rates are apt to decline in a slump, thus encouraging orders for capital goods, and to rise in a boom. But these variations have proved inadequate to even out the cycle. It is possible that no variations, however great, would be adequate. There is a very good reason why actual variations should not be.

The current rate of interest depends on the current valuation of titles to a specified future income. That current valuation depends in large measure on what the future valuation is expected to be. The current *yield* of titles depends both on the current rate of interest derived from the present valuation, and on the relation of the current valuation to the prospective future valuations.

For this reason, if the current rate of interest varies, either this variation must be expected to be permanent, or else the current yield will be very different from the current rate of interest. For example, if a present fall in the rate of interest is expected to be permanent, the expected yield will fall in the same way as the rate of interest; but if the rate of interest is expected to rise again in the future, the future valuation of titles to income will be lower than their current valuation, so that the expected yield will be very low. And there is no reason to suppose that the market will deliberately arrange matters, so that those large variations in yield occur which are necessary to bring about *temporary* changes in the rate of interest. When large changes in the rate of interest do occur, this is because the market has a change of mind of substantial importance about the prospect of interest rates over a period of time much longer than the immediate phase of the cycle.

Again the crucial point at which the demand for capital goods falls off may be considered. To allow production to go forward steadily, it is at least necessary that a substantial drop in the rate of interest should occur within the 'breathing space'. Only so can the construction of capital goods be maintained constant, despite the fall in the prospective rate of increase of consumption, and only so, therefore, can the major depression be averted. But unless the present drop in demand is very quickly followed by a complete revision of opinion by the market covering the whole course of future events extending over a longer period than the cycle, the rate of interest cannot drop very much; for, if it did, the present yield of titles, based on a comparison of their present valuation with their expected future valuation, would fall below zero. And why should any one buy titles at a price which makes their expected yield a minus quantity? The rate of interest (long-term) is prevented from fluctuating as much as would be required in order to keep the progress of production steady by the fact that it depends on long-term considerations.

The matter may be put in this way. Suppose the short-term rate of interest to fluctuate so much that, if only the long-term rate fluctuated equally, a steady advance of production would be maintained. Suppose this fluctuation in the short-term rate to be foreseen. Long-term stocks are not likely to be valued at such a level that their yield is less than the average of short-term rates taken over the foreseeable future. They will probably be valued so as to yield somewhat more owing to their inferior liquidity. Suppose for simplicity that this undervaluation of long-dated stocks is constant throughout the cycle. On this hypothesis the fluctuation in the rate of interest on long-dated stocks will be very small. It will fall a little in the slump, merely on account of the fact that the immediately impending bad period, because nearer, is more heavily weighted in the average.

For the long-term rate of interest to vary as much as is required, short-term rates would have to vary many times more; and this is impossible, since it would require, for long-term rates anywhere near as low as those to which we are accustomed, a large minus figure for short-term rates during the bad years. Actually the long-term rate probably varies more than the strict argument here set forth requires, partly because the undervaluation for illiquidity may become less in the slump and also because the market is so much in the dark about the future that it is unduly swayed by the immediate situation. The strict argument, none the less, gives a good reason why the long-term rate may be expected not to vary enough, as in fact it does not, for cyclical depressions to be averted.

It may have occurred to the reader that in the later sections of this book, in which the amount of investment and its relation to the prospective rate of advance have been discussed, the considerations regarding the stability of our régime, founded on a study of the Crusoe state, played but a subordinate part. Was this early section, indeed, irrelevant? Was it merely a device to hold the reader's attention, by directing his suspicions to a wrong quarter? No; the analysis of the stabilizing elements in a modern society there set out is indispensable to the general theory.

Consider the fluctuation of prices, which occurs in the cycle. Many have thought that this is the primary cause of the trouble, and when pressed for a reason why that itself should occur, have sought to cast suspicion on the unfortunate bankers. Those miscreants have caused prices to fluctuate by mismanaging the monetary system!

Now he would be a foolish man who would seek to deny that the price fluctuation is intimately connected with the output fluctuation, which is the central phenomenon of the cycle. But how connected? The argument regarding the interaction of the motives of savers and the motives of those who give orders for additional capital goods has no direct reference to the price level. In the slump, stocks of consumable goods tend to become redundant, orders are reduced and income runs down until the actions of the two parties are in accord; in the boom the reverse happens. The fluctuation of income and output is the inevitable result of the difference of motives on which the decisions of the two parties are based.

The total amount of output of capital and consumable goods is the aggregate of those undertaken, by a large number of different individuals, each with no direct private interest in the equation of new capital construction to the volume of saving in the community in general. The action of each is the result of the impact of the general situation on him personally. The fluctuation of prices measures the resistance of the individuals to change. It provides the force necessary to make them change their level of output and so behave that their resultant output is what is required to make capital construction equal to saving. Thus the price fluctuation is still in the centre of the picture; but it is no longer represented as the ultimate cause, and the banking community is exonerated.

The ultimate cause of the cycle is the peculiar relation of the creation of new capital to saving. The price fluctuation is the mechanism by which this ultimate cause operates upon individual units to induce them to carry out the variations in output required. If all output were undertaken by cartels rigidly organized, not indeed to maximize their profit, but to secure that the prices of their products remained absolutely constant, then the ultimate cause might operate to produce the output fluctuation without this intermediate mechanism. As demand declined (or increased) the cartels would be quite willing to let output decline (or increase) without resistance. The price fluctuation represents what remains in our complex system of man's natural determination to continue earning his livelihood, even when conditions become less favourable, and of his unwillingness on the other hand to be rushed into overwork. An analysis of how these natural impulses still operate in our modern society was therefore highly relevant.

That analysis also served to throw some light on the causes of profit fluctuation in the course of the cycle. It suggested that it was unnecessary to look to time-lags or miscalculations on the part of business men as its main cause, and that the profit fluctuation was an inevitable *effect* of the output fluctuation itself.

From one point of view the profit fluctuation is a thing to be deplored, like so many other features of the cycle. From another it is seen to perform a valuable service. For if output is to fluctuate—and, so long as the divergent motives of savers and of those who order capital goods are allowed unimpeded play, it appears that it must continue to do so—the amplitude of output fluctuation is diminished by profit fluctuation. When the demand for saving runs down, the diminution of income and output required to effect the curtailment of saving will be less, if during the diminution there is a shift of income away from the profit-takers, who are the big savers. And conversely in the boom.

The rise and decline of activity and its present level are determined by dynamic forces. But all the while the static forces remain. The phenomena of price- and profit-fluctuation represent the resistance of the static to the dynamic forces. The prevailing error in cycle analysis heretofore has been the mistaking these phenomena of resistance for the true causes of the cycle.

This essay thus claims to present a precise and definite diagnosis of the cycle. But much more remains to be done. The diagnosis is only presented in broad outline. No attempt has been made to reduce it to quantitative terms, so that it might form a basis for prediction as to the probable duration of cycles or the amplitude of impending fluctuations. If the arguments set forth are accepted we may be confident that another great reverse will occur. But we are no nearer knowing when it will occur. Nor is it at all certain that we shall recognize it when it has already begun. In the early part of 1930 there was no general agreement among experts whether a major recession was impending; it is not clear that in the early phases of the next slump we shall be any better placed in that respect.

Yet if the qualitative argument were accepted we should be better placed in another respect. The nightmarish quality of the events of 1929–32 was largely due to the fact that no one was able to give a sensible and coherent account of what it was that was happening or why it was happening. There was the widest divergence of opinion as to what type of action was likely to be remedial. The most intelligent comment, to which a small number of highly enlightened and far-seeing persons were able to rise, was that the current events did in fact constitute the downward phase of a trade cycle and could be classed with phenomena already well known and analysed in treatises on trade fluctuation. But the great mass of experts, journalists, and publicists did not even get so far; they were more concerned with special *ad hoc* causes. Even the reference back to other trade recessions did not carry the matter of diagnosis very far; for it was well known that the theory of this topic was still quite rudimentary.

II. *Stable Money*

By far the most respectable proposal for eliminating or mitigating trade fluctuation is that for providing a stable[1] medium of exchange. Its merits may be set forth.

In the first place it is extremely simple, at least in its broad outline. The concept is easy to grasp. And although, when it comes to a precise definition of stability, difficulties and ambiguities appear above the surface, yet in the actual world we are so far removed from a monetary stability that would satisfy any definition whatsoever, that there is work enough to do in removing gross fluctuations of value before the need arises for getting down to disputes about niceties.

Secondly, the project is one which may be justified on

---

[1] Throughout this section the word stable is used in the sense of *not fluctuating*; it is not intended to preclude a steady secular upward or downward trend in the value of money. Cf. the criticism of the narrower objective of a *constant* price-level on pp. 117–18.

the broadest grounds and would be approved by any one of scientific disposition, whether he were versed in the subtleties of economic theory or not. Money is used as a measure of value. That which is used as a measure of magnitudes of a certain kind should not contain a fluctuating amount of that magnitude itself. Otherwise its use as a measure is reduced to nonsense. This is a matter of plain common sense and should commend itself to all. It does not depend on any particular economic or monetary doctrine, the validity of which might be open to dispute. It is self-evident and its correctitude may be established on grounds which are logically prior to and independent of all economic theories and controversies. Acquisition of a stable measure would seem to be desirable, quite apart from any remedial effect that it might have on the trade cycle. It would provide in the economic sphere what must be regarded as a most rudimentary requirement in any field in which quantitative methods are used.

Thirdly, fluctuations of economic activity have been so regularly connected with fluctuations in the value of money that, again quite apart from particular doctrines as to the precise nature of their causal relationship, it seems overwhelmingly probable that there is some connexion between them. This argument gives no assurance that if monetary fluctuation were removed trade fluctuation would automatically be removed also. But it does strongly point to the desirability of trying the experiment of monetary stability.

Finally, coming in the last resort to the arguments of economists, a large variety of reasons have been adduced from different points of view why monetary instability might be expected to cause trade fluctuation. I do not propose to give a catalogue of these reasons. Taken together they make a notable case. The consensus of opinion among economists on this score is remarkable.

If anything further is needed to recommend this experiment, one may cite the feebleness of the arguments of

those who are opposed to it. Men require some tangible
basis such as gold to give them confidence in their money.
There have been great abuses of the system of incon-
vertible paper money in the past; there were French
assignats and the German marks. Without the solid
anchorage of gold we should be at the mercy of unscrupu-
lous politicians, who are capable of anything and might
produce the utmost chaos. These arguments are those
of pure conservatism and obscurantism. Human nature
being what it is, we cannot hope to improve our condition.
In human or social matters it is too much to ask for a tool,
which in any of the physical technologies would be the
first and most elementary requirement. All this in an age
when politicians are being allowed to tinker with the
economic system in every manner of way. Duties, subsidies, quotas, restrictions, compulsory cartelizations are
doled out with lavish profusion in a casual and haphazard
manner, unsupported by any argument from general principle, on no coherent plan and with no defined objective,
and with no reasons adduced, that will bear a moment's
consideration, why they are likely, broadly and in the long
run, to be beneficial. Against this is set a demand, simple,
precise, well-based on logic and common sense, supported
by the great majority of professional experts. Yet nothing
is done about it. What is the explanation?

I conceive it to be this. In these matters practical men
need to be advised, not in terms of an objective but of the
practical measures required to secure it. And in this
matter there is not that simplicity and lack of ambiguity
which we find in the objective itself. Stout upholders of
the Quantity Theory might indeed affirm that the means
are as simple as the end. The value of money depends on
the quantity in existence; it is only necessary to regulate
the quantity of money in circulation in a certain manner,
and its value may be precisely controlled. But even starting from this perhaps over-simple point of view the matter
ramifies. Money nowadays consists mainly of banking

deposits. The quantity of these can be varied through the banks varying their terms of lending. But suppose that borrowers are unresponsive The central bank may under-take open-market operations. How far will these have to be carried? The joint-stock banks must follow suit. In the United States they have recently refused to do so. How can they expand credit if the public is reluctant? By undertaking open-market operations themselves. How far can they go in this? What proportion of their assets can they safely hold in the form of investments? May their position not become dangerous before money has been sufficiently increased to prevent appreciation of its value in a slump? They may have serious fears that they are imperilling their liquidity. But, it will be said, this is a small matter compared with the importance of a stable medium of exchange. Still, the security of their depositors must be the paramount consideration of these banks; they are merely joint-stock companies and concerned with their own solvency and their profit-earning capacity. Must they be given a government guarantee, or even taken over by the state in the interest of a national credit policy for stable money? And what of the foreign-exchange position?

Thus, even if we look at the matter through the eyes of quantity theorists, the *means* of securing the objective of stable money may not be altogether easy of encompassing. From the point of view of the practical man the request for stable money does not give such a clear lead as the request for a duty on imported steel. The issues at stake are not, perhaps, more complex than a wise control of milk production, whatever that may mean. But then the interests affected by monetary reform are more widely ramified. Moreover, in the case of milk, the beneficiaries, the interests which have to be organized, and the parties clamouring for action, are mainly one and the same. Whereas in the case of monetary reform, it is the econo-mists who clamour for action, a large and complex group of financial interests which has to be organized, and the community as a whole which benefits. Moreover, the party which clamours for action in this case being merely academic and having no personal interest at stake, is irresponsible and discredits itself by public disputes over trifles.

None the less, the demand for stable money is so eminently respectable and so firmly grounded on good reasoning that in the long run one may be sure that it will be met. But how long will the run be? What is required is some machinery for translating the general demand into definite proposals which practical men can understand and execute. How is that machinery to come into existence? Whence is the initiative for setting it up to come? From the side of the economists? But there is the danger that in an inquiry organized by themselves their energies would rapidly be frittered away in disputes of great academic interest but of little importance to the main issue. From the side of the politicians? But so long as the demand for a stable money is presented in abstract terms they are not likely to be converted, and, if not converted, they will not take the necessary initiative. So the matter stands. The conclusion is depressing enough. Who will have sufficient inspiration and wisdom to overcome the obstacles?

I have laid stress on the desirability of attaining this objective. I preach the gospel of stable money. But it is my particular duty to consider it in relation to the diagnosis of the trade cycle which has been presented in this essay. The conclusion of this consideration will be that the problem of securing stable money is likely to be somewhat more intractable than the simple-minded quantity theorists suppose. This conclusion has two aspects. It adds to the gloom which the foregoing paragraphs may have engendered, but it also introduces a ray of hope. It adds to the gloom because if the necessary means are still more complex than has already been suggested, we would seem to be still farther removed from being likely to persuade the practical men.

It introduces a ray of hope by suggesting that after all the practical men are not so blind. They may have been immune to the suggestion that they should take up the doctrine of stable money, not simply because they have been crass and obstinate or mere vote-catchers, but because they have felt in their bones that the kind of means suggested for securing stable money would not work. Looking about, as presumably they do, for wares to peddle to the electorate, some inner voice, the product of some deep unconscious mental process, may have been warning them that there was no line here which would do them credit, or no line which they could undertake to deliver. Not that they examined it and found it wanting; but out of the corner of their eye they may have caught a glimpse of something or vaguely heard some murmurs from economists and have been told by their unconscious mind, endowed with its own curious kind of wisdom, not to turn aside and waste their time about it.

What does our diagnosis suggest about stable money? Certainly not that it is undesirable, for, if a steady advance could be achieved, this would involve some form of monetary stability. But it suggests that the obstacles, which the achievement of a steady advance and stable money alike have to overcome, are very serious. This is no reason for not continuing to advocate stable money. All right-minded men should continue to cry loudly for stable money, since this is required by principles more far-reaching, simple, and self-evident than any construction of specifically monetary theory. But if the doctrines of this essay are indeed true, then the Royal Commission on ways and means to stable money would find themselves confronted with precisely the obstacles suggested by this analysis and would have dutifully to find a method of overcoming them. Consequently, if the following paragraphs imply some scepticism with regard to the means usually advanced for achieving stable money, this must not be taken to imply any defalcation on my part from that great cause.

It is the doctrine of this essay that the dynamic determinants are bound from time to time, in the absence of oft-repeated pieces of good fortune, to decree a full recession. Experience suggests that, when this happens, a considerable fall in prices is necessary to overcome the force of the static stabilizers. It is the dynamic determinants and not some forces connected with the effective quantity of money (MV) that *cause* the recession. When the recession occurs, prices have to fall because of the static stabilizers; and they will fall however much the market may be flooded with new money. The movement of prices is thus caused by the operation of the dynamic determinants.

Monetary recipes designed to stabilize prices will only succeed in doing so if they operate with sufficient force on the dynamic determinants. Can they be made to do so? In this section it may be well to delimit monetary recipes to those which can be carried out by the central and other banks. Public works and budgetary operations have recently come to be regarded, rightly, as an integral part of monetary policy. They will be considered in the following section. Here attention is confined to bank-rate policy and open-market operations.

When the dynamic determinants decree a recession, a sufficient fall in the rate of interest to restimulate investment is required. If this fall can be secured within what has been called the breathing space, a full recession may be avoided. But if the breathing space is already overpassed, it is unlikely that a fall of the interest rate to zero could prevent a recession to the bottom. Our first problem then is to find statistical means for distinguishing a genuine breathing space from ephemeral and accidental fluctuations in global figures, which might merely be due to the lumpiness and discontinuity of the industrial process or to local divergencies. This may be extremely difficult to achieve. Yet we may be sure, for reasons adduced on p. 113, that if the breathing space is allowed to go by, no manipulation of the interest rate will avail to stem the downward movement.

Next, can banking policy secure the required movement of the interest rate? That the banks can operate very effectively on short-term rates need not be disputed. But it is a matter of legitimate doubt whether the stimulus to net investment due to a fall of short-term rates is of appreciable importance. Long-term rates depend primarily on the prevailing view as to what the future has in store. How can this view be modified in the short period of the breathing space? If it is known that a great slump is impending, a decline of the interest rate may be precipitated. But it is the object of the authorities to prevent this slump. It is most important, moreover, that a slump should not be anticipated, for the injury to net investment due to such a prospect is likely to be greater than the benefit provided by a fall in the rate of interest.

Mr. Keynes in his recent volume has taken a somewhat optimistic view as to the plasticity of the long-term rate under the influence of monetary policy. If only the banks, by open-market operations, supply the public with a sufficient amount of money, they can reduce the price, which is required to make people sacrifice liquidity and invest in loans, to any level they please. In principle this may be so. But if a very great increase of money is required to reduce the rate of interest by a minute amount, the policy may become impracticable. If the prevailing view is that the rate will be at a certain level a few years hence, a small fall of the rate below this level reduces the prospective yield of fixed interest-bearing securities to zero, and for any rate below this it is better to hold money. At this point the elasticity of the demand for fixed interest securities may become almost infinite, or, to put it otherwise, the banks may be able to inject an unlimited amount of money through open-market operations without being able to raise the price of fixed interest-bearing securities appreciably. And at this point the monetary recipe can do no more. If the fall in the long-term rate so far secured by open-market operations is insufficient to hold up the recession decreed by the dynamic determinants, no further injection of money will prevent the price-level falling.

Strong mental resistance to the acceptance of this view may be encountered. Surely, it may be urged, it is mere nonsense to suppose that it is impossible to depreciate money by sufficiently increasing its quantity. History may be cited in which great increases in the quantity of money have regularly been accompanied by a great inflation of prices. Are we to suppose the law, widely vouched for by experience, by which a great increase of money produces a rise of prices, to be suddenly suspended in order to accord with a new-fangled theory of the trade cycle? It would be rash to be over-dogmatic. Friends of humanity cannot but hope that at the onset of the next depression the banks of the world will attempt the experiment of increasing the quantity of money on a heroic scale and that the experiment will be successful. But there are serious reasons for doubting it.

The argument from the examples of history may be rebutted. In all the cases which may be cited the injection was not an experiment designed to raise prices, but the consequence of a great increase of investment—usually arising from an unbalanced budget—to finance a war or a revolution. This increase of investment operating through the multiplier might be expected to raise prices in accordance with the principles enunciated in Chapter II, Section III. At first the rise might be moderate, but in a time of full activity, once the pressure for raising wages becomes strong, the vicious circle of rising wages and prices may gain rapid acceleration. In these cases we are in the presence of some cause other than monetary policy *in the first instance* tending to produce a great acceleration of investment and activity generally. In these circumstances a lax monetary policy may intensify the upward movement of prices. But at the onset of a cyclical depression this non-monetary factor, which is the actuating cause, is absent.

And what of the argument from common sense that it *must* be possible to depreciate the value of money by sufficiently increasing its quantity? It is necessary to consider how the increase is effected. It will be remembered that the means supposed are open-market operations by the banks. Now it is not denied that these operations in so far as they succeed in reducing interest rates and stimulating activity will have some effect on prices. But apart from this consequence the open-market operations considered in and by themselves only provide new money to be held on capital account. The banks and the public merely swap capital assets, the banks providing a more liquid form and the public surrendering a less liquid form. If the effect on the rate of interest is ruled out of consideration, there is no force tending to put this money into active circulation or to cause it to operate upon the prices of commodities. This injection of new money by open-market operations, this swapping between banks and the general public of forms of capital asset, is indeed a mere pseudo-inflation and cannot be expected to have the same effect on the price-level as a true inflation.

In this matter, as often happens, progress along a certain line of analysis has engendered a complementary error. It used to be imagined that the *fons et origo* of inflation was the use of the printing press. Recognition that in the modern world banking deposits were a more important element in the monetary system than banknotes led to the perfectly correct view that a government would as surely provoke inflation if it met its expenses by borrowing from the banks as if it used its own printing-press. So, it was explained, during the War it was the expansion of banking deposits against Treasury Bills or other forms of government indebtedness that was the root cause of inflation; the expansion of the note issue was merely consequential and governed by the needs of the community for small change in a period when inflation was occurring owing to the expansion of credit. Thus it was argued that the expansion of credit was the essence of inflation. But, it was said, it is not necessary to inflation that the government be the borrower. Any expansion of banking credit, e.g. by open-market operations, may equally well be regarded as inflationary. Only the last step in this chain of reasoning was wrong.

Looking at the matter more deeply, it appears too simple to say that the expansion of banking deposits against government indebtedness is what precisely constitutes inflation, though it may be closely connected with it. The most essential element is the expenditure by the government of sums vastly in excess of what it takes in taxation. This constitutes a great block of net investment. How is the necessary saving provided? Partly, perhaps, by an economy campaign; further by the high level of activity providing the community with a global income from which they would normally save more than usual; then, in so far as these two sources are insufficient, through the rise of prices and consequent shift to profit. Given the excess of government expenditure over tax receipts, prices are bound to rise sufficiently to produce an excess of business receipts over costs sufficient to meet the needs of the government. Then the race of wages and prices may further add to the inflation of prices. But wages never catch up and in the nature of the case they cannot; for, if they did, the shift to profit would be insufficient to provide the necessary saving.

Do the banks, then, play no part in the inflation? They do play a part. If they allowed no expansion of credit, there would be a great shortage of money to meet the high monetary value of turnover, and interest rates would tend to rise to a very high level. This would severely check investment generally. This might reduce the total amount of saving required and mitigate the rise of prices necessary to secure it. But with the very high government

investment there would probably all the same be a severe
inflation of prices.

The quintessence of the inflation is the excess of government expenditure over tax receipts.[1] The expansion of
banking credit merely removes from the field the deflationary influence that very high interest rates could exert
in other parts of the economic system; but this would
probably not be of substantial importance by comparison
with the very powerful inflationary force of government
activity.

In the case of an expansion of banking credit through
open-market operations designed to keep up the level of
prices in a slump, the quintessence of inflation is absent.
The mere increase in the quantity of money is of no significance in relation to the price-level, except in so far as
a consequential fall in the rate of interest exerts an inflationary influence.

Yet there may be a residue of mental resistance. Surely
it is nonsense to deny that it is impossible to keep the
value of money steady in relation to a group of commodities. What about the case of gold? Many nations over
long terms of years have succeeded in keeping their money
absolutely constant in terms of gold. But if in gold, why
not in terms of any other commodity or of a group of
commodities? It is true that at times countries have been
'driven off' the gold standard; but, it might be contended,
that has only been because they were not absolutely determined to take all steps, however drastic, to maintain it.
And in the crucial case under discussion, it is not a question of preventing the currency depreciating in terms of a
given standard, but of preventing it appreciating. Who
has ever heard of a country being compelled against its
own will to allow its currency to appreciate in terms of gold?
There have been instances, like that of Sweden during

---

[1] High expenditure even if covered by taxation may be inflationary in
so far as the additional taxes are found otherwise than by a sufficient cut
in current consumption.

the War, of countries choosing to let their currency so
appreciate. But what country has ever been unable to avoid
its currency rising in gold value? If not in gold value, why
in terms of other things? Indeed the large group of commodities should be easier to maintain as a standard, since
gold is subject to considerable variations in value in terms
of other things, which the large group is not.

This query is very much to the point, and the reply to
it will throw light on our contention. Those who adduce
the example of gold must admit that if there is one maxim,
upon which all who have studied the working of the gold
standard would insist, it is this, that the only way in which
a gold standard can be successfully maintained is by
allowing free convertibility of the currency both into and
out of gold. Suspend the compulsory selling or buying
prices, suspend the right to melt or close the mint, and the
market price of gold will immediately begin to fluctuate.
No one, I believe, has ever seriously contended that mere
use of the discount rate, without provisions for convertibility, would keep the price of gold within the gold-points.
Is it not the lesson that a similar convertibility into and out
of goods could alone suffice to preserve a goods standard?
A commodity standard has been said to be an extension to
n commodities of Marshall's plan for symmetallism. But
it was assuredly part of Marshall's plan that the currency
authority should hold stocks of gold and silver and be
obliged to convert the currency into and out of the prescribed weight of gold and silver on demand.

The view that prices could be sustained by such a plan
is not in disaccord with our fundamental theory of the
cycle. For when the dynamic determinants decreed a
recession and a consequent fall of general prices, the
monetary authority by being willing to buy the basketful
of commodities at the stated price would keep production going. The residue of output unsaleable in the
market at a remunerative rate would be planted on the
monetary authority. Its stocks of goods would continue

to accumulate until the dynamic determinants decreed a renewed advance. This would involve the extension on a heroic scale of the policy of the Federal Farm Board in the United States.

It might be said that this plan has only to be mentioned to be rejected as absurd. One's view as to its absurdity depends on how seriously one regards the evils of a major trade depression, not only economic, but social and political, and what sacrifices one is prepared to undergo in order to avoid those evils. In the past the reserve of gold in the central bank has not been wholly disconnected from the idea of a war chest; an ample stock of cereals, rubber, pig-iron, copper, &c., might be even more useful in that respect. I do not think it shows a good sense of proportion to dismiss the project out of hand.

Yet it must be admitted that there are very grave difficulties. In the construction of general index numbers the prices of basic raw materials, which can be ascertained from quotations in organized markets, are generally used. One is apt, therefore, to think of a commodity standard in terms of these, and in the foregoing paragraph there was a reference to the monetary authority holding stocks of grain, rubber, &c. It is not clear, however, that the maintenance of the prices of these basic materials is what is required in a country mainly engaged in the production of finished consumable goods and capital goods. To elaborate a theory of what might be expected to happen to the prices of these, if the price-level of the basic materials was maintained, would be to stray too far into the realm of hypothesis and conjecture. It is not by any means apparent that such price maintenance would suffice to stem the action of the dynamic determinants when these decreed a recession in the output of the goods on which the country was primarily engaged. It is true that such maintenance would in the event of a world recession and a fall of world prices automatically depress the value of its currency in terms of other currencies and so stimulate the active items in its foreign balance. This, however, involves the danger of reprisals of progressive severity. And it would be over-dogmatic to assert that the stimulus to active items would be sufficient to prevent the recession. But, it might be suggested, why not base the commodity standard not on basic materials but on the commodities, in the production of which the country is mainly engaged? This would entail the monetary authority being willing to hold a mis-cellaneous collection of goods, such as motor-cars whose type was rapidly becoming obsolete, ladies' frocks, all sorts of goods usually made to order, even ships and houses. At this point the project clearly does become a little far-fetched.

It may be well at this juncture to consider another kindred plan for stabilization, especially associated with the name of Professor Irving Fisher. He has put forward a proposal for securing a commodity standard, which does not involve the holding of actual commodities. The currency is to be convertible on demand into gold, not, however, into a fixed and unalterable quantity of gold, but into such a quantity of gold as will buy a constant quantity of commodities. Thus it is a project for secur-ing stable commodity prices by marking up or down the statutory price of gold. What is the essential nature of this plan? If it were adopted on a world scale it would manifestly be inadequate to fulfil the task required. One might mark up the price of gold sky-high. This would clearly be an enormous stimulus to investment in gold mining. But would the increase in this one branch of investment be sufficient to restore investment generally to the required level? The proposition in essence is that if you mark up the price of one particular commodity suffi-ciently, this will drag up the prices of commodities gene-rally. Is this to be believed? The doctrine should be applicable to any commodity, for in this regard gold has no particular virtue. Can the general level of commodity prices be sustained by marking up the price of one particular commodity, of wool, of iron-ore, of shellac, to a sufficiently high level?

The expedient might be more effective if adopted by one country only, particularly by a small country, in an unregulated world. For then, since the action of this particular country would not alter the relation of gold to other commodities in the world as a whole, the marking up of gold in terms of its currency would automatically entail the marking up of other commodities. What is this expedient in essence? It is none other than the old plan of raising internal prices by means of exchange depreciation. Its effectiveness would depend on the degree to which the active items in the foreign balance would be stimulated by these means. It would, like the expedient already mentioned, probably provoke reprisals. And not altogether unjustifiably. For it is of its nature predatory. It involves an attempt to use the external world as a lever to hoist up the country's own prosperity without regard to the depressing effect which the process may have on the world outside. It can hardly be recommended at a time when greater international monetary co-operation is urgently required.

This is not to say that the doctrine of the good neighbour should preclude a country from allowing its foreign exchange to depreciate. If a country is resolutely determined to combat trade depression by all the means in its power, depreciation of its currency may be the inevitable consequence of the measures it takes. It is impossible to lay too much emphasis on the distinction between a depreciation which occurs as the natural and inevitable result of strenuous internal measures undertaken by a country to secure higher activity and greater employment at home, and depreciation artificially engineered as a means of stimulating activity.

If the next depression is to be taken seriously by authorities in this country and combated by adequate measures it is very much to be hoped that the employment of the

Exchange Equalization Account as a method of regulating the Foreign Exchange position may be retained and not replaced by a return to the gold standard or any other kind of fixed parity. For once a parity is established and other countries have come to rely upon its stability, there is bound to be strong pressure to retain it, even when departure from it has become expedient. There is pressure from the authority, whether it be the Bank of England or an official body, which has been responsible for its maintenance and developed for that function a technique, in which it has acquired a vested interest or, shall we say, for which it has come to have a deep-rooted affection that cannot be lightly flouted. And there is the pressure due to the dictates of honour. If foreigners have acquired monetary assets in the country on the implicit understanding that they will be able to withdraw them at par, honour requires that some efforts should be made to preserve that par. That pressure to preserve the *status quo* may be fatal to the timely application of recovery measures; the technical authority will throw its weight into resisting those measures if it conceives, as it will rightly conceive, that they may jeopardize its technical task of maintaining the parity. When it is remembered that it is of vital importance that the recuperative measures be timely and quick, that, if they are to succeed, it is probably essential that they should be executed within the 'breathing-space', the grave danger of allowing a fixed parity to come into existence with vested interests growing up around it is apparent.

There is a corollary. If recuperative measures are likely to entail exchange depreciation, it is most important that all foreign countries should appreciate the nature of the distinction referred to above. They must understand that the depreciation is a consequence of the internal measures and is not being used as a weapon to stimulate exports. In order that they may understand this it is necessary that the Exchange Account should disclose its proceedings and publish periodical balance-sheets. For only so can other countries know what is the nature of the depreciation that is occurring. If the account is losing foreign funds it is clear that the fall in the exchange rate is forced upon it. But if it depresses the exchange in the absence of any outward movement, if it engineers a fall by itself buying foreign funds, it may rightly be held up to blame. It may be too much to hope that even in the former eventuality other countries will refrain altogether from retaliatory measures. But a clear appreciation of what is happening should preserve international goodwill and an atmosphere favourable to co-operation.

This suggests another argument in favour of the flexible system. Under it, gentle upward and downward movements may continually be allowed to occur. Experience shows that they are of negligible inconvenience to foreign trade. In that case there need be no sudden depreciation. At times the downward pressure may become stronger. There need be no crucial moment at which a demand for retaliatory measures abroad arises. But once a parity is fixed, then the crucial moment occurs when that parity is broken.

The burden of this argument has been to suggest scepticism about the possibility of securing stable prices by purely banking methods. The one method which might be expected to be effective, namely the provision for convertibility of the currency into and out of commodities, is so strange and novel and presents such violent practical difficulties that it would probably be injudicious to press for its adoption. Our analysis suggests that more orthodox methods alone are not likely to succeed. But where so little is known and so little has been seriously tried it would be quite wrong to press the scepticism too far. The issues at stake are great. Nothing should be said which would sap the willingness of the authorities to experiment with orthodox banking remedies to the limit of their powers.

III. *Public Works and Public Finance*

Public works have recently been much discussed as a means of dealing with the unemployment problem. Their advocates have been enthusiastic, but have met with a large measure of hostility and scepticism based on sturdy common sense. This is because the best grounds on which they may be supported have not been widely understood.

On the one hand there is the naïve and perhaps sentimental view, 'Here are these poor fellows out of work; we must really give them something to do. Do not raise pettifogging objections based on economic sophistication. There is a plain human problem. Conscience demands that we should deal with it promptly and by all the means at our disposal. If there are adverse economic repercussions these must be dealt with as they arise. Meanwhile there is work to be done, which may or may not be financially self-supporting, but which anyhow is useful and will be of some benefit. Let us set the men to it and maintain their morale by giving them a job, which is their birthright, and so ease our own consciences.' This is the kind of view which naturally and properly provokes a dogged resistance. 'That is all very well. But we have an economic system, which is supposed to provide work through the laws of supply and demand. Men make goods which they are prepared to take off each other's hands by the process of exchange. If you interfere with this system by setting them to make goods which others are not prepared to buy, where will the matter end? By all means have public works which can be shown to be truly remunerative. But once you start creating work for the sake of giving employment, you are embarking on a process that will ultimately disrupt the whole system. In fact you are implying that we have no system. The right method of curing unemployment must be based on an examination of the system and consist of remedying any defect that is found, oiling the wheels, so that it may function as it should more

efficiently. Do you intend to scrap the system and introduce full-bodied socialism? If you do, you should say
so. But in that case you are most unlikely to cure unemployment by this partial tinkering. The employment
given by your public works will probably be offset by a
further decline in the efficiency of the system itself with
a consequent decline of employment given by private
enterprise. Do not forget the vicious circle of the Speenhamland days.'

There is no doubt that this is a healthy and rational
retort. If the sole case for public works were that stated,
the rejoinder would carry conviction. But it is not the sole
case or the proper case.

First we may consider the matter in terms of stable
money. In the last section it was hinted that those who
consider the matter purely in terms of monetary reform
have ceased to confine their attention to recipes which
may be provided by the banks acting on their own. The
operations of government have a powerful effect on the
monetary situation and, in order to secure stable money,
it might prove necessary to harness the forces which it
controls. Actually our system has not provided a stable
money. But the provision of stable money, by appropriate
means, cannot be regarded as an action subversive of the
system. Surely it must be agreed that it would be an
added perfection, and not a mere ornamental flourish
either, but a perfection that would enable the system to
work more smoothly after its own fashion. If public works
can be shown to be the simplest and most efficient means
of securing monetary stability, then the grounds for their
advocacy are entirely altered and arguments referring to
the bottomless pit of Speenhamland, the ever-extending
vicious circle of relief, become quite beside the point.

From the simple monetary point of view the argument
can be put thus. In a depression it is desired to sustain prices by increasing the quantity of the circulating
medium. The banks endeavour to do this by making their

terms of lending more favourable, in the hope that they will thus be able to increase their loans and so the deposits of the people. But suppose that private enterprise is not stimulated, or insufficiently stimulated, to borrow. Then let the government come in and fill the gap; let the government engender that extra demand for loans the insufficiency of which is preventing the banks from adequately increasing the circulating medium and so sustaining the price-level. The answer given to this line of reasoning is that even if the public is reluctant to drink, the banks may none the less increase the quantity of circulating medium by open-market operations. Mr. Hawtrey has argued in this manner. If the real object of public works is to constitute an additional demand for loans and so to enable the banks to expand credit and sustain the price-level, it is really quite unnecessary to go to all this trouble, since the banks can expand credit directly through the open market without the intervention of the government. On this view public works are an unnecessary piece of ritual to enable the banks to do what they could do quite simply on their own.[1]

The force of this objection depends on a view of the effect of open-market operations which has already been dealt with. The new money created by an expansion of credit will only have a direct effect on the price-level if it proceeds directly into the income stream as when the government borrows for public works or industry borrows for new capital outlay. The new money injected by open-market operations merely finds its way into capital accounts and has no direct effect upon the price-level. Thus it may be claimed that public works, financed by borrowing, would have an efficacy in raising the price-level that open-market operations lack.

But, if the argument of the foregoing section concerning the essential nature of inflation is correct, it is not neces-

[1] Cf. R. G. Hawtrey, 'Public Expenditure and the Demand for Labour', *Economica*, March 1925.

sary that the government should borrow from the *banks* for public works. The inflationary effect will be equally present if it borrows from the general public. It should not, of course, finance the works by taxation, for then no new net investment is created.[1] All that the banks need do, to assist the government policy, is to keep credit sufficiently expanded to prevent any rise of interest rates. If the public works are inaugurated with a view to sustaining prices, still more if they are introduced to bring about reflation, it is quite likely that there will be no need for the banks to inject new money in order to keep interest rates down, for the reflationary effect of public works will bring money out of capital accounts into active circulation once more. None the less the banks must be vigilant to see that there is no tendency for interest rates to rise in consequence of the expanding activity, and must be prepared to co-operate with the government to the extent of injecting sufficient new credit through the open market to prevent this.

Thus public works may be seen to take their place as a useful mechanism for sustaining prices. It is necessary to consider them in relation to our theory of the trade cycle.

It may be well to recall what happens at the onset of a depression. A simplified version consisting of four stages may be set down. (1) Some fall in the amount of net investment (operation of the dynamic determinants). (2) In consequence, some fall in consumption (the Multiplier). (3) In consequence, a great fall in the amount of net investment (the Relation). (4) In consequence, a further fall in consumption (the Multiplier). Things are going further forward merrily, when the totality of forces, which determine what amount of net investment is needed in relation to the demands of an advancing economy, decree some decline in net investment. The consequence of this is that, since people will insist on saving a certain propor-

[1] Public works financed by taxation may not be completely ineffective, since high taxation may reduce the propensity to save.

tion of a certain income, there is a deficiency of purchasing power, and income as a whole tends to run down. But when income runs down the greater part of current net investment is no longer required. Then income has to run down much farther. Now the ideal thing that could happen at the first stage would be such a fall in the rate of interest as would keep net investment at its old level and altogether obviate the other three stages which are so disastrous. Unfortunately the long-term rate of interest, dependent as it is on long period prospects, cannot be jockeyed about to suit the exigencies of the short period, whatever the banks may do. And because this cannot happen we have the absurd and tragic result that the whole level of activity has to be drastically curtailed till net investment reaches 'the bottom', which may not be very far above zero, and activity and profit become so low that a correspondingly small amount is saved. A system which brings about this fantastic result cannot be said to be fulfilling its function properly. Nothing has gone wrong with the productive power of the community or its willingness to work, nor have its needs become less clamant. There is no fundamental reason why it should not continue to progress in production and wealth. But the mechanism so works that it cannot turn the corner from the condition in which at a certain rate of interest a given amount of net investment is required to a condition in which at the same rate a somewhat smaller amount is required, without being pushed down to a very low level of activity and having slowly to build up from there. Put otherwise, the long-term rate of interest certainly will not of its own and probably cannot be made to move downwards for a short period sufficiently far in response to a short-period change in the situation; and the consequence of its not doing so is a full depression.

Now this is clearly a defect of the system; to seek means of remedying it is not to seek to undermine the system. Public works are recommended as such a means; let us

hear, therefore, no more of Speenhamland in this connexion.

If a sufficient volume of Public Works can be arranged
to begin during the 'breathing-space', the volume of net
investment can be sustained, or, more strictly, the current
rate of increase of net investment can be sustained, and the
deleterious consequences of its decline can be avoided. It
is clearly of mighty importance that the inauguration of
public works should be timely and speedy. For if they
can be started during the 'breathing-space', disbursements
of comparatively moderate value may suffice to maintain
regular advance. But if the system has already run down
a considerable way towards the bottom, works on a heroic
scale would be necessary to bring it up again. Anything
that was practicable would in that case probably only be
a small palliative. The attempt to secure stability would
have failed.

Now it is often argued that the project of making public
works an equilibrating factor in the trade cycle is really
utopian, on the ground that with our existing machinery
public works take a long time to plan, that they are related
to broad questions of public policy and are not a tap to be
turned on and off at will. When the execution of a great
plan had been begun it would be most wasteful and often
quite impracticable suddenly to cease work upon it at the
behest of the trade cycle experts.

This point is one of serious importance. The moral is
that our whole attitude to public works should be altered.
It is quite useless to abide in the vague hope that if and
when a recession occurs, then, if the view of the economists
prevails, some useful public works may be found to help
matters out. What is required is that a Public Works
Planning Commission be set up here and now. It should
be given a threefold task. (1) It should endeavour to
formulate statistical tests for ascertaining the advent of a
'breathing-space' Since it is essential that the execution
of its plans should be timely, it is important that it should

know in advance how to determine when the time for action has arrived. (2) Of all public works likely to be undertaken in the next decade it should sort out those the time of the inauguration of which can be adjusted to trade cycle needs. (3) It should have regard to the transfer problem. Since it will be required to act before unemployment has become widespread, it is important that it should know in advance how to acquire the labour and other factors of production required without delay. Since there are reasons for supposing that the next slump will supervene while unemployment is still considerable, this problem may prove less intricate than it would otherwise be. The transfer question may have an important influence on the type of works selected for the plan.

This Commission should have a large selection of possible projects to draw upon, since many may prove unsuitable with regard to timing and with regard to the kind of labour required. It should therefore be empowered to take cognizance not only of the activities of the central government, but also of those of local authorities and of public and semi-public bodies (e.g. London Transport, Water Boards, &c.). This implies investigation and possibly interference over a wide range. With loyal co-operation advisory powers might suffice. But compulsory powers must not be ruled out. This might well involve considerable friction with bodies jealous of their own autonomy and far-reaching adjustments of a constitutional and financial kind. The task of the Commission would be no light one. Parliament should devote much time to defining its duties and powers.

In a period of improving trade this project sounds bizarre and far-fetched. There is little likelihood of its being immediately adopted. The trouble about the trade cycle is that the evils of depression are forgotten in the revival and most people console themselves with the hope that they will not recur. When they do recur and the feeling that the government should do something begins to run high, it is too late to employ effective remedies, for the breathing-space is past. It is probably too much to hope that anything effective will be done at the onset of the next slump. The most optimistic view that can reasonably be held is that something might be done to avert the slump after next. Before the last slump practical men were not warned what to expect. If they are warned this time in vain, in the period before the slump after next they may be reminded that they were warned and took no heed, and so perhaps be persuaded to give ear.

The plan for a Commission here outlined is a far-reaching one; most intricate questions concerning the relations of various authorities are involved; many existing financial regulations concerning borrowing powers and sinking funds would have to be readjusted if the remedy was to be effectively applied. Many a hornets' nest would be raised. The task of the Minister for co-ordinating the National Defence Services pales into insignificance beside the thorny problems facing our Commission. And what is it all for? To cope with a problematic slump, which may never occur, which has merely been conjured up by the too vivid imagination of the economists? But another major war may never occur. Yet we are hastening on with our defence arrangements. Wars do not recur with ineluctable regularity after certain intervals. But depressions do. A reasonable man could bet with greater confidence on a major slump occurring within the next ten years than a major war, although the former might well be the cause of the latter. This is the crucial point. Unless the trade cycle is treated by the responsible authorities as a well-established fact, and unless far-reaching plans are organized on that basis, we are not likely to avert the ravages of the depression. Is it worth while to do so? Is it worth while to incur administrative costs and still greater administrative bothers, to avert a catastrophe which, though highly probable, cannot be said to be absolutely certain? That depends on how serious a view is taken of the consequences of a major slump. If it is true that the political turmoil throughout the world in the last five years, including the present state of international affairs in Europe (1936), may be directly traced to the economic disasters of 1929 to 1932, there can be no doubt about the answer. We in England cannot, of course, avert a world slump. But in these days economic recipes (e.g. quotas!) spread by imitation from country to country quickly, and a well-conceived plan, seen to be effective in England, might be copied elsewhere very rapidly.

I have argued that it is not enough to entertain a vague hope that, when another slump occurs, something may be done to mitigate it through public works; but that determined and serious-minded steps should immediately be taken to plan ahead. But in fact the present position is considerably worse than that of vague hope. The responsible authorities are probably not yet convinced that public works can in fact act as an equilibrating force. This may be illustrated from the events of recent years. In 1931, when the depression was at its height, public works were ruthlessly curtailed in the interests of economy. Since then the atmosphere has steadily become milder, restrictive regulations have been relaxed, slum clearance schemes initiated, and generally a more sympathetic attitude adopted towards capital projects, on the ground that we are beginning to be able to afford them once again. What does this mean? That there is still deeply embedded in the minds of the authorities the view that public works are a luxury which the country can afford if it is fairly prosperous, but which must be rigorously cut down in times of adversity. This is the exact opposite of the equilibrating doctrine. Public authority is merely following in the footsteps of private enterprise, allowing itself to be swayed by the same psychological influences, increasing net investment when private enterprise increases it and cutting it down when private enterprise cuts it down. In reality the fact that the country can 'afford' to spend more is a reason for spending less. Until this paradox is grasped we may look in vain for any effective action to cure the trade cycle.

The full restorative effect of public works depends on their being financed by a borrowing. An alternative mechanism that has been suggested for preventing the appreciation of money is the financing of the ordinary current expenditure of government by public borrowing. These recipes clearly have a family resemblance.

Advocates of the latter are, like advocates of public works, confronted with a strong tendency to resistance on grounds which are also healthy and, as far as they go, sound. It is the natural inclination of a government seeking popularity to disburse as much money and to take away in taxation as little as it possibly can. If this inclination were allowed full play it would lead to financial chaos. Consequently in order to be armed against the force of its own inclination it is necessary that the government should feel it to be immoral and pernicious to show a deficit in its finances. Sound budgeting is rightly regarded as the hallmark of responsible and mature government. States which lapse from deficit to deficit and from deficit to repudiation are held to be, and usually are, backward. The credit of their government is undermined and the community suffers accordingly. It has not been easy to secure the enforcement of the principles of sound budgeting; their successful and secure establishment marks an advance in the art of government. When, therefore, it is suggested that after all a budgetary deficit may in certain circumstances be expedient, this sounds, at first blush, like a retrograde proposal, a relapse into moral laxity. One great department in which economists and sages and the leaders of public opinion have very properly believed that they could quite safely speak in the person of education, of reason itself, has been that of sound public finance. Are the effects of this persistent and strenuous effort of education to be undone? Are the flood-gates to be opened wide?

The first task of those who believe that a budgetary deficit may at times be a valuable recipe should be to guard themselves against this misconception. They should only seek to introduce their ideas if the general principle of financial solvency is already taken for granted. That principle must be the foundation. Upon that basis they propose to introduce certain more subtle considerations. Thus they should make it clear that neither the urgent importance of certain public projects nor a widespread clamour for tax remission could possibly justify a government in spending beyond its means. Such an expenditure is to be justified by the phase of the trade cycle and by that alone. Is it possible to introduce this subtlety without undermining the basic principle itself? I think that it is taking too low a view of democracy to suppose that this is impossible.

To put an experiment of this sort upon a proper footing the authority for allowing such expenditure should be devolved upon an expert body concerned with the study of trade-cycle conditions, and having no political bias nor concern with the prospect of general elections. The Chancellor of the Exchequer should be responsible for balancing his budget in the ordinary way. But at certain times the Expert Body, acting entirely on its own initiative, would notify the Chancellor that it would put at his disposal certain funds which he could treat as general revenue. So far as he was concerned this accretion of funds would be a blessing coming *ab extra*, like some abnormally high yield of death duties, which he could use for his own purposes, but of which he would in no circumstances be entitled to ask for more. Such a body might appropriately be called Commissioners of the Currency Equalization Account.

Before proceeding it is necessary to consider the economics of budgetary deficits in relation to the trade cycle. The effect of public works inaugurated during the breathing-space would be to maintain a given level or steady increase of total net investment and so prevent the adverse

repercussion on the whole of economic activity which a
recession in the volume of private net investment would
otherwise entail. If net investment is maintained at a
proper level there is no reason why the general level of
activity should recede. The effect of a budgetary deficit
is similar but in certain respects different. Formal definitions may be correctly framed so that a budgetary deficit
counts as so much net investment; this treatment brings
out the similarity while obscuring the differences. The
matter may be looked at somewhat more realistically.
Public works involve the creation of certain new capital
goods, which must be added to those produced by private
enterprise to make up the total of current net investment.
A budgetary deficit on current account raises the level of
expenditure on consumption above what it would otherwise be. A decline of net investment normally entails a
decline of consumption in accordance with the multiplier.
But if, when the incomes of those engaged in producing
capital goods recede by reason of the decline of net investment, the *total* money income of the community is none
the less caused to increase at its normal rate by a budgetary
deficit, consumption may continue to increase. Thus the
secondary and tertiary effects of the decline of net investment may be avoided. If the normal increase of consumption is maintained, a small decline of net investment need
not be followed by a decline to the bottom. And if the
budgetary deficit is sufficiently large, consumption may be
further increased so as to absorb some of those thrown out
of work by the small decline of net investment, if transfer
is possible.

As in the case of public works, it is desirable that the
budgetary deficit should be quick and timely, that it
should, in fact, occur within the breathing-space. But this
would entail a drastic revision of our budgetary system.
It would not be sufficient for the Chancellor of the Exchequer to wait for Budget Day before taking into account
funds credited to him by the Currency Equalization

Account, and then to introduce tax remissions which might not affect the purchasing power of the community for another six months or more. Tax remissions should be introduced as soon as the Currency Equalization Account makes its funds available, and they should be so chosen as to make their effect on purchasing power felt immediately. The Chancellor of the Exchequer should introduce what might be called a reverse supplementary budget. This would involve a departure from time-honoured habits and would be, to that extent, obnoxious. The justification for the proposal is again the seriousness and urgency of the problem which it is intended to solve.

It might be hoped that a well-timed variation in the volume of public works would be a sufficiently powerful equilibrating factor to prevent full depressions and that the expedient of a deficit on current account would not be necessary. It may be so. But the more apprehensive one is of the difficulty of rapidly varying the volume of public works without great waste, owing to the need of long-period planning, the more probable one must hold it to be that the second expedient ought to be brought in aid also. But this expedient will only be superior to public works in efficiency, if it is possible to introduce highly expeditious methods of generating and removing budgetary deficiencies.

A word must be said about confidence. The deficiency may lack curative effect if it gives rise to considerable loss of confidence. For this loss may have its own adverse effect on net investment, the volume of which depends on the judgements of individuals with regard to the maintenance of progress in future, and it may also have an adverse effect on consumption, if the deficiency makes people fearful of future stability and therefore cautious and thrifty. There is also the danger that the rate of interest may be affected. It is therefore highly important that this policy should not be put into operation as a last desperate expedient, but as the inevitable consequence of a predetermined policy, vouched for by authority, well authenticated and recognized by the public to be such. Preliminary work of education is necessary. This is a further reason for setting up the Currency Equalization Account at an early stage, endowing it with all possible authority, pomp, and dignity, and constituting it in such a manner as to command the highest possible public confidence.

For trade-cycle purposes, it is not enough that budgetary deficiencies should be capable of being generated and eliminated with rapidity; this will be of no avail unless the consequential change in the purchasing power of the public as rapidly takes effect in a demand for consumable goods. If the budgetary deficiency is generated by a tax remission, the taxes should be chosen with this end in view. It is probable that taxes which fall upon the poor are most suitable for this purpose. For the expenditure of the poor is constantly held down by an actual shortage of cash. If prices of working-class goods fall through a remission of indirect taxation, most of the money saved is likely to find its way fairly quickly into the purchase of other goods. The connexion between the current receipts and current expenditure of the super-tax paying class is, as we have already had reason to notice in another connexion, looser. They are accustomed to variation in their cash receipts owing to a number of causes, and their standard of life tends to be planned with a view to long-period solvency; a windfall receipt coming to them would be registered with satisfaction, but would be unlikely to lead to any great change in their level of expenditure. It might be argued that super-taxpayers would feel themselves better off as a result of super-tax remission and would react to the feeling by carrying out some long-wished-for improvement in their mode of living. But it must be remembered that at the time when the remission is made there is no good reason to suppose that it will not have to be withdrawn after a year or two; and this is known; they would naturally be extremely cautious in making any long-period plan on the strength of it. Those who normally live up to their income are apt to be in continual danger of outrunning it; the windfall receipt would probably be regarded as giving a welcome assurance that they are more likely to be on the right side and would therefore make little difference, if any, to their immediate level of consumption. Those who are endeavouring to tuck away some savings would be likely to throw in the windfall receipt as well.

Thus the weakness of public deficiencies as an equilibrating factor is that there is no guarantee that they will have a proportionate effect on purchasing power. The public deficiency might have to be much larger than the computed deficiency of purchasing power in order to be effective in preventing a recession. If the United States Veterans' Bonus is considered from this point of view, there is reason to fear that its inflationary effect will be not too great but too small to be a powerfully stimulating influence.

So far the deficiency has been supposed to be produced by tax remission. It might also be produced by an increase of current expenditure without any corresponding increase of taxation. Many expedients might be devised by the Treasury or the Cabinet itself working in close co-operation with the Currency Equalization Account. For instance, it might be part of the government programme to increase its expenditure on some form of social service; if this could be introduced at a time when the Currency Account declared itself desirous of transferring funds and the rise of taxation required to finance the new expenditure could be postponed to a later date, the deficiency so produced would be likely to exert its maximum effect. For the beneficiaries of the scheme would rightly treat their new income as permanent and therefore tend to spend a considerable proportion of it, while, taxes not yet being raised, no one would have reason for retrenchment. Taxes would be raised subsequently when it was no longer necessary to give an artificial stimulus to purchasing power, or, possibly, would not have to be raised at all, the necessary revenue coming in from the increased yield of existing taxes at a later date. Any such plan implies that trade-cycle policy is occupying a central place in the thoughts of the Cabinet about home affairs. And so it should.

Of financial expedients, which have actually been put into operation in this country, the one most conformable to the doctrines of this chapter was that by which the Unemployment Insurance Fund drew upon its surplus or ran into debt in a depression. By this system an actual deficiency automatically came into existence in a depression. Unfortunately, most of the virtue was taken out of it, first by the transference of transitional payments to the Exchequer, and secondly by the sudden insistence in 1931 that the Insurance Fund must balance in a year of deep depression. It is now generally believed that the old system, wrongly condemned in 1931, mitigated the severity of the depression in this country, and that the subsequent reversal of policy would have considerably enhanced it, had not counteracting factors come to our aid at the time, the depreciation of sterling, the revival of confidence, and a measure of protection. The change of policy was partly due to the misguided ideas of the government. But, even had the government been more enlightened, it might have been necessary, owing to the state of public opinion and the loss of confidence which borrowing for unemployment was causing, that is, owing to the misguided ideas of people generally. This means that for the earlier system to work it is necessary not only that the government should be converted to the new ideas, but also that public opinion should be educated up to them. With intelligent leadership this should not be difficult.

Reference has already been made to the fact that the expenditure of well-to-do people depends not so much on their actual current receipts as on the estimate they form, based not only on the immediate present but on prospects in the near future, as to how well off they are. The looseness of the link between receipts and expenditure makes the problem in hand more intractable. The existence of an organized stock exchange is liable to make this problem still more acute.

This appears to be the appropriate point at which to refer to the Wall Street boom, which culminated in 1929. It gave all shareholders a very inflated idea of their own wealth and probably caused many of them to live on a higher scale than they would have done had they regarded their actual income only. If this was so, it was natural to expect that, when the boom in stock prices burst, there would be a great deflation of purchasing power. This would quickly bring into operation the forces, which have already been analysed, that make for a full depression. And since annual net investment was extremely high in the United States the depression was proportionately severe. Thus producers and traders in the United States suffered from the reaction to a boom for which they, as such, had not been responsible. And the whole world suffered. This is not to say that the dynamic determinants operating in the ordinary way might not sooner or later have decreed a full recession. But in the face of the necessity for liquidating the inflated condition of the stock market, the problem of averting depression during the breathing-space was far more difficult. The recession of expenditure in the early stages was due not only to the decline of income caused by such decline of net investment as the dynamic determinants decreed, but also to the general sense of impoverishment consequent upon the decline of stock-market prices. There was a much larger gap in purchasing power to be filled up, if a full recession was to be avoided, than there would have been but for the special stock-market factor.

There was at the time, and still is, a feeling that if a steady economic advance is to be achieved, a great and

unstable inflation of stock-market prices must be prevented. Some might be inclined to dismiss this problem
as arising out of the special characteristics of the American
temperament. This is probably too optimistic a view.
Temperament may have played its part. But the objective
fact must be taken into account, that the United States
had reached a level of general wealth in which it was possible and natural that stock-exchange speculation should
be very widespread. If the advance of wealth, rendered
possible by the progress of technology, is maintained, this
country and others will soon be approaching a similar
position. It is too facile to hope that level-headedness will
alone suffice to save them from this penalty of being
wealthy.

The problem of the Stock Exchange is one that may
have to be dealt with specifically. In the critical years,
1927-9, eyes in the United States were turned to the
Federal Reserve System as the institution whose proper
duty it was to cope with the trouble. There are good
reasons, however, for doubting whether the central bank
is the appropriate body to deal with this problem; and the
hesitation and half-heartedness with which the Federal
Reserve System tackled it indicated that this doubt
was present to it. It was authorized by law to regulate
credit with a view to producing stable conditions for
industry and trade. That the Wall Street boom was a
menace to that stability cannot be doubted. But if credit
policy is regarded as the appropriate method of curbing
the exuberance of Stock Exchange speculators, there is
danger that a conflict may arise between the policy required for that object and the interest rate policy which
would conduce to the steady advance of production under
the influence of the dynamic determinants. Such a conflict was probably present in those critical years.

Production figures suggest that the breathing-space
antecedent to the full depression began in July 1929. Yet
the Stock Exchange boom continued to rage for another

three months. What was to be done? It is arguable, and the point has been suggested by Mr. Hawtrey, that, if a recession in production was to be averted, easy money should have been introduced in July.[1] Yet a body with one eye fixed upon the Stock Exchange situation could not possibly do this. The dilemma was a nasty one. There is no reason in the nature of things for supposing that it will not recur.

The lesson appears to be that it is not possible to rely upon the same instrument, credit policy, for controlling the rate of interest and regulating the Stock Exchange. If a choice must be made between the two objects for which credit policy may be used, priority must be given to the former. Experience teaches that credit policy may be at least partly effective in controlling the interest rate, while there is no reason to suppose that it could control the level of share prices. Control of the interest rate is in the tradition of central banking, and no other method readily occurs to the mind for securing this end. It remains true, however, that it is also of vital importance to prevent Stock Exchange inflation. There may be no alternative to imposing direct control in this sphere by legal restrictions on dealing. This opens wide questions which require careful study.

It has been suggested that the Stock Exchange inflation was not unconnected with some kind of inflation in the field of production and commerce itself. It is doubtful if this suggestion is well founded. There was no general rise of prices in commodity markets. It is contended that prices should have fallen in the face of rapidly increasing productivity and that they were artificially sustained by the Federal Reserve System. If prices were higher than they should have been, none the less there was consider-

[1] See R. G. Hawtrey, *The Art of Central Banking*, ch. 2, p. 81, last paragraph. Mr. Hawtrey, it is true, does not make it quite clear whether he would have commenced relaxation after July, or merely have made it more vigorous in October.

able unemployment in this period. Is the moral of this contention that an economic system, such as that of the United States, should not be allowed to work at full capacity, and that it cannot be allowed so to do without making a Stock Exchange inflation and a consequent full recession inevitable?

It is necessary to look more deeply into the American situation in these years. Capital and consumable goods were being produced in profusion, but not at a rate that strained the productive capacity of the country, since unemployment was still considerable. Is there any sense in saying in these circumstances that there was over-production? Surely not. Was there a lack of balance between capital and consumable output? It cannot be said that the Americans were living beyond their means, in the sense of consuming too large a proportion of total output, since the provision of capital goods in this period was somewhat above the normal. Can it be said that there was an excessive production of capital goods, that net investment had reached a level which made recession inevitable, whatever remedies might be applied? But what does this signify?

If we look at the production figures, a case can be made for the view that there was some lack of balance consisting in an excessive production of capital goods. If, on the other hand, we look at the disposal of income, the opposite conclusion is indicated. For it seems that, given their incomes, people would not have spent so much, had they not taken that rosy view of their own fortunes which was caused by the Stock Exchange boom. It is on that contention that the gravamen of the case against allowing the Stock Exchange boom depends. Only if it is true that, when that boom came to an end, people were bound to restrict expenditure was it necessary to consider the boom as a serious menace to the maintenance of progress. If the boom might come to an end and people continue to spend as before, then the boom should be regarded as a harmless excrescence on the system, which would cause many people indeed to burn their fingers, but which need not be treated as involving a serious threat to the maintenance of industrial activity. The view that this might have happened hardly appears plausible.

Now, if that view is rejected, the proposition follows inevitably that during the boom people were spending more on consumption than they would have done, given their incomes, without the stimulus it provided. They were led on to spend more than they would otherwise have done by a phenomenon which could not continue indefinitely. They were in fact spending more than people with their level of income and their temperament would normally do. There was a lack of balance between saving and spending, consisting of an abnormally high degree of spending. The lack of balance here suggested is in flagrant opposition to that suggested by the production figures. But for the Stock Exchange inflation people would have saved more than they did; but according to the production figures, as things were, they were saving more than was consistent with a proper balance between the output of capital and of consumable goods in industry; they were saving too much in spite of the fact that there was a strong adventitious and temporary influence inducing them to spend more than they would naturally have been inclined do to. The conclusion to which these arguments lead is ominous.

This essay has been concerned with an analysis of the trade cycle, of the inevitable succession of boom and depression. In a boom we have seen that the production of capital goods tends to become abnormally high and in a depression abnormally low. In a boom the abnormal amount of saving required is forthcoming, partly indeed because activity and income are high and people tend to save a larger proportion of a high income, and partly because there is a shift to profit, a larger proportion of which is saved. Thus the abnormally large amount of capital required in a boom is found. Now these phenomena are not obviously inconsistent with the possibility of achieving a condition of *steady* advance and a high level of activity. It is true that this latter condition would not require such a high level of capital construction as the abnormally rapid advance of a boom (the Relation); but then if profits were not inflated one might hope that the community as a whole would spend a larger proportion of its income and that there would be no tendency to over-saving. The high level of construction in a boom and the shift to profit are connected by the fact that the high level of profit is required to provide the saving necessary to the high level of construction. If only we could get into a condition of high but not rapidly advancing activity, then, it might be hoped, the high level of construction and the inflation of profit could both be dispensed with.

The American experience points in a different direction. For there it appears that the condition of fairly high activity and fairly high construction was marked not by a great inflation of industrial profit causing the community as a whole to save a larger proportion of their income than usual, but by a great inflation of Stock Exchange prices, causing them to spend a larger proportion of their income than usual. In retrospect the progressive inflation of Stock Exchange prices may be regarded as an indispensable part of the mechanism for the maintenance of high activity in that period; for as soon as it broke there was bound to be a deficient demand for consumable goods. These events strongly point to the view, which is strictly outside the scope of this essay, that in a country as far advanced in prosperity as the United States behind the phenomena of the trade cycle there may be a long-run tendency to over-saving. This accords with a conclusion which Mr. Keynes reaches by a different process of reasoning.

It might be urged that the supply of saving can always be adjusted to the demand for it by the rate of interest. How does this fit with the American experience? How can we suppose that the high but by no means excessively high level of activity in the United States in the years 1925-9 could have been maintained without the stimulating effect of the Stock Exchange inflation? By a higher rate of interest than actually obtained? Clearly not, for with a higher rate of interest and in the absence of capital appreciation on the Stock Exchange, people would undoubtedly have saved more, and the amount required for capital construction would have been less. A recession would have been inevitable. By a lower rate of interest? This might have deflected money from the stream of saving, but it is doubtful if it would have deflected as much money as the condition of rosy optimism engendered by the appreciation of equity prices. It might have stimulated more capital construction, but it must be remembered that the exuberant confidence of the times, which was not unconnected with the Wall Street appreciation, was a great inducement to embark upon investment in capital goods, and this may have been more important than nice calculations of 3 or 5 per cent. The fact is that the events on the Stock Exchange constituted a powerful force making both for a high level of capital construction and a high level of consumption; it is doubtful whether a rate of interest, however low, could have exerted an equally powerful influence. We shall return to this point.

The immediate moral is that the Stock Exchange position should be controlled by other means than credit policy. If a very low rate of interest is to be regarded as an alternative to a Stock Exchange boom as a method of averting depression, then the central bank must not be impeded in its low-rate policy by the duty of killing a Stock Exchange boom. Some other means must be found for achieving the latter aim.

Much has been said about public borrowing for public works or to meet a deficiency on current account. What of the reverse process? Or is the pressure of government finance to be all in an inflationary direction? The reverse

process consists in the repayment of public debt by allocations to sinking funds. A strong sinking fund policy
appears to be called for in the upward phase of the cycle,
in order to keep down the total burden of public indebtedness. Thus the proposed policy of equilibration may be
defined as that of public borrowing during the depression
and repayment during the boom, or, more strictly, since
the object of the policy is to prevent a recession to the
bottom from occurring, as that of borrowing during the
breathing-space, whenever a recession threatens, and repayment at other times. This definition is logical and
reasonable; but it is beset with serious difficulties.

The policy might be put into operation smoothly if the
starting-point were a condition of high activity. Unfortunately, owing to the ravages of the recent depression, that
cannot be our starting-point now.

It is generally agreed that in Great Britain at least we
have already (in 1936) advanced a considerable way on the
upward curve of the cycle. Does this mean that we should
recommend a restriction of public works and the repayment of debt on a generous scale? In view of the unemployment position it seems hardly human to propose
a policy having a tendency to restrict the rate of advance.
Are we bound by the formula to do so? Surely not, if the
formula is conditional on the starting-point being one of
full activity. We should impose no obstacles until that
state is reached, and then bring into operation our equilibrating policy.

The consequences of this must be frankly faced. It is
quite probable that the dynamic determinants will decree
a recession, as they did in 1929, before a condition which
can be properly described as one of full activity is reached.
Then a great increase of public indebtedness will be required. If the policy is then successful, the subsequent
condition may still be too unsatisfactory to warrant deflationary measures. How long shall we have to wait
before the other side of the policy can be introduced and

the volume of indebtedness be considerably cut down?
How many times will the stimulus have to be applied
before a brake can be put on? What of the growing burden
of interest charges? What of the credit of a government
the indebtedness of which is steadily increasing?

These thoughts may be unduly gloomy. It is possible
that we are not so far removed as we seem to be from a
condition of full activity. There is a difference of opinion
as to how far present unemployment would be reduced if
labour were redistributed among districts and trades. As
a complement to the regulation of demand, vigorous
measures ought to be adopted to deal with the problem
of transferring labour. With regard to the reduction of
unemployment which such a transfer policy could bring
about it is necessary to remain agnostic.

It is possible that the one-sided character of the equilibrating remedy, as it presents itself to us here and now,
is not entirely due to the accident of our present starting-
point. It is possible that the nature of that starting-point
is no accident, but is connected with a general tendency on
the part of a wealthy community to save too much. This
is a view to which, it has been suggested, the American
experience strongly points. It is a matter on which it
would be most rash to be dogmatic at this stage. It can
only be put to the test by the execution of experiments on
the lines suggested in this chapter. If the view is correct,
it may be necessary to maintain public works and public
borrowing as permanent processes to be intensified from
time to time when the determinants threaten a depression.

What then of the accumulating interest burden? It is
premature to be too much alarmed by this. It may happen
that the experiment of evening out the cycle would show
that in the long run the system is capable, without external
stimulus, of running to full capacity. In this event it will
ultimately prove possible to reduce indebtedness by a
strong sinking-fund policy in good years. I should not,
however, be honest with the reader, if I concealed my own

opinion that this is unlikely to be the case. Since it may not be the case, the possibility of a progressive growth of the interest burden must be briefly considered. Even if this turned out to be the unavoidable consequence of the stabilizing experiment, there is no need for excessive alarm.

It is well to take stock at this point. Consideration of the problem of the cycle suggested the expedient of a budgetary deficiency to be introduced during the breathing-space. In order to safeguard the principle of sound budgeting it was proposed that an independent commission should have sole responsibility for initiating the policy by reference to the phase of the trade cycle. Consideration of the state of widespread unemployment in a recovering world and an analysis of conditions in the U.S. in the period 1925–9 suggested that there might be a chronic tendency to over-saving. Though this matter lies outside the scope of our analysis, it was necessary, for the sake of frankness, to refer to it in connexion with the practical proposal for a Currency Equalization Commission. For clearly their form of instructions would have to be somewhat different according as whether they were expected (a) to balance deficiencies incurred at successive 'breathing-spaces' by surpluses gathered at other times, or (b) to allow the total burden of indebtedness to grow. For the sake of symmetry, as also to soothe the susceptibilities of financiers of the old-fashioned type, it would be agreeable to choose the former alternative. Yet if there is in fact a chronic tendency of over-saving, which is responsible for serious and present distress, it would be wrong to make our choice for reasons such as those.

The difficulty is that our knowledge is insufficient for a pronouncement here and now whether there is such a tendency. Further experience and experimentation are necessary. Since we are in fact ignorant, it would be proper to allow latitude in our instructions to the Commission commensurate with our ignorance. If our diagnosis of the trade cycle is correct, such latitude should not be dangerous. For the evil which they should be charged with averting is specific, namely a recession to 'the bottom', which will occur if and when consumption fails to advance. They are to be charged with securing that consumption does advance. They should further be instructed to collect such surpluses in the interval as were found by experience not to precipitate the state of affairs which it was their duty to avert. The experience of the Commission should itself provide the knowledge which we lack.

It might be objected that such vague instructions would hardly give it the authority necessary to coerce a Chancellor of the Exchequer to disgorge surpluses. It might not. In that case the situation would be no worse than it is at present; and it would probably be a little better, since it may be presumed that they would exert *some* influence in keeping the Chancellor on his toes. If they did not exert the full influence, which they would wish to, that would not be fatal. For it is no part of the doctrine of this volume that the evils of the depression are mainly due to the 'excesses' of the preceding boom.

There are, however, two conditions in which the Commission might be given absolute power, as against the Chancellor, to demand a surplus, namely, (i) if wage-earners in the face of a rising cost of living were obtaining wage advances in excess of any probable increase in their efficiency—some crude yardstick might be devised to measure this—or (ii) if on balance in the system, or perhaps in industries chosen as representative because they occupied a middle position in respect of expansion or contraction, there was a high level of unfilled vacancies. In this case the exchequer accounts would be automatically debited with the amount named by the Commission, and, if the Chancellor failed to make this up, he would be publicly pilloried as not having balanced his budget. These suggestions presuppose that the government has been converted to the desirability of preventing depressions, and is willing to co-operate loyally.

It remains to consider whether, in the event of it proving undesirable to secure sufficient surpluses to balance deficiencies, there would be good grounds for alarm at the growing burden of indebtedness. In the first place the growth of capital claims in some form is the inevitable result of the right and willingness to save. If every year there is a considerable volume of net saving, then the volume of outstanding capital claims must grow. This may or may not be regarded as a burden on the future; it is a burden which the future will be called upon to bear so long as the right of the individual to accumulate wealth is recognized.

The special features of the proposed stimulus by the public authorities which might give ground for alarm are, (i) that it would involve too large a volume of capital claims taking a fixed interest-bearing form, (ii) that too large a proportion would be guaranteed by the government, (iii) that it might involve a progressively troublesome transfer problem, namely, how to get the money from one set of pockets, the taxpayer's, into another, those of the holders of government securities, and (iv) that, in the event of government borrowing to finance a deficiency on current account, there would be no capital assets corresponding to the capital claims.

(i) Prima facie the fixed interest-bearing claims should involve no greater burden on the future, since the prospective return on equities is higher in proportion to the risk that such capital claims may become worthless. Indeed, if it is true that the bearers of risk succeed in the long run in extracting from the community a special 'reward for risk-bearing', the future will have a smaller burden to carry if a higher proportion of capital claims is of a fixed interest-bearing kind. The real danger of an excessive burden of fixed interest indebtedness is connected with the possibility of catastrophic falls of prices. But it is the object of the proposed system to prevent such catastrophic falls. If the system failed to achieve its main object, then some readjustment of capital claims might prove necessary. But that readjustment is equally likely to be necessary, if a succession of major depressions occurs in future and no special measures to remedy them are taken.

(ii) The government guarantee may be represented as imposing an extra burden in the future on the ground that it makes it less likely that future generations will rid themselves by default of a portion of the capital claims arising from the past. An argument analogous to that advanced at the beginning of the foregoing paragraph may be used here also. If the government is expected to be less likely to default than private borrowers, if, in fact, its credit is better, the interest rate with which the future is burdened, in respect of a given advance of capital now, will be correspondingly lower. What the future is likely to lose on the swings, it will gain on the roundabouts.

(iii) It is quite impossible to forecast the magnitude of the transfer problem, since the magnitude of operations required to maintain a steady advance is itself unknown. So much thinking has recently been directed to the herculean task of raising communities from the trough of a great depression, that it is possible that an exaggerated idea prevails as to the scale of operations which would be required, if only they could be carried out promptly in the breathing-space. Furthermore, it is possible that borrowing could be undertaken, without making the transfer problem acute, on a much greater scale than people are in the habit of imagining. Science has not yet exhausted its resources or its fund of surprises. It is not unreasonable to plan with the expectation that the level of real income will continue to advance. Even with all the maladjustments due to cyclical depressions, an upward secular trend of income per head has been maintained in the past. An acute transfer problem should not arise if the amount to be transferred to bond holders does not increase more rapidly than the level of total income. At the present level of the National Debt in England approximately

£80 million could be borrowed annually for every one per cent. increase of national income without going beyond this limit. If the borrowing allowed by this formula could be concentrated wholly or in part in the periods when the dynamic determinants were behaving badly, the funds available for manœuvre in times of crisis would be truly magnificent. Something more modest might well suffice. It must be admitted, however, that if the downward movement of population indicated by existing birth rates is realized, the basis of this calculation would be seriously upset within two decades. The present trend of population does indeed make nonsense not only of the existing National Debt, but of all our hopes for the future. None the less it is a contingency that must be faced. If it is the case that owing to the population trend output is destined to increase at a far smaller rate than in past years or even not to increase at all, the problem which these measures are designed to solve, the disposal of savings, will be *pro tanto* more acute. The amount of saving per head is not likely to decline, but on the contrary to grow, and in the ordinary way most of it would then have to be absorbed through an increase in the amount of capital used per unit of output. But it is by no means clear that this increase will be an important factor. Thus the same contingency that is likely to make the transfer problem troublesome is also likely to make the use of the kind of expedient here proposed indispensable to the maintenance of full activity. It would in the circumstances be necessary to rely on measures to secure that the rate of interest is reduced to the lowest possible level and the burden of interest commitments to a minimum.

(iv) The fourth ground of alarm appears on the face of it to be the most serious. Yet I think it may be dissipated by further reflection. It must be reiterated here that the problem of accumulating indebtedness will only become a real one, if it is in fact true that, however the rate of interest may be manipulated, there is a secular tendency for a wealthy community to save too much. If there is no such tendency, our proposed remedy will not entail the accumulation of indebtedness. If there is such a tendency, what is the moral?

What is the essence of the position? Under the existing system men have the right to accumulate. Individualists have long cherished the hope that the power to accumulate may become more and more widely diffused, with growing wealth, until it reaches every fit and able-bodied individual. We are still far from that ideal condition. But we are moving in that direction. What is to happen if the value, which people at a given level of income choose to accumulate, exceeds the value, which can by any manner of means be embodied in capital goods that are useful to people at that same level of income? Are we to abolish the right to accumulate? About the discouragement of accumulation something will be said presently. It may be that we shall rapidly move towards a form of socialism, of which such an abolition is the natural corollary. Our arguments, however, are related to the present system or some intermediate system short of complete socialism. One alternative to abolishing the right to accumulate is to tolerate a permanent and perhaps intensifying condition of under-demand and under-employment. The other is that proposed here. If people wish to accumulate more in the form of claims than they need in the form of capital goods, let them receive liens on the future income of the community to the benefit of the existing taxpayer and at the expense of future taxpayers. This means that the agents responsible for future production will have to pay over some proportion of their growing income to those who have in the past accumulated such liens.

There appears to be something disagreeable in this proposal to enlarge the rentier element. Is it more disagreeable than the waste and misery of under-employment on the one hand, or the hasty abolition of the right to accumulate on the other? Is it not better that we should build up a rentier position than that we should be unable to afford to do so? Moreover a tendency to excessive saving should make it possible to push the rate of interest down to a nominal level, so that the rentier position would not be a strong one.[1] The disagreeable flavour of this proposal may be connected with the idea of the accumulation of large fortunes and an intensification of inequality. But in fact large fortunes are seldom built up by thrift alone. Still less would this be possible with a very low rate of interest. The question of levelling out wealth is another matter. A plea may be made even to the extreme socialist in favour of the right to accumulate. There is something irresistibly attractive in the individualist's picture of each man with his own little hoard. Are we to cast it away just when we are within measurable distance of securing a really democratic diffusion of this power? Private hoards may be thought of as an indispensable condition of real liberty. A socialist régime might supply secure jobs to all. But what of the man who says 'I hate your office and its red tape; I hate your faces and your ways and your bureaucratic insults; you think I am a good engineer, but I think I am a poet; you think my poetry is worthless, but I beg to differ.' If he prefers his garret to an up-to-date flat and car and annual jaunt to Boulogne, it would be agreeable if he were free to choose on the basis of his little hoard. Or, less ambitiously, the hoard might be regarded as a fund for emergencies, giving him the power to quarrel with the authorities if he wished to, and to stand up for his own rights, the modern equivalent of the cottager's five acres and a cow.

In any case the abolition of private property is not likely to occur in the near future. If there really is a tendency to save too much, the practical alternatives may be under-employment or the accumulation of state indebtedness. One school of thought would wish to cut the Gordian knot by the issue of interest-free credit. This proposal takes

[1] Cf. J. M. Keynes's *General Theory of Unemployment, Interest and Prices*, p. 276.

many forms, and the arguments on which it is based usually show bewildering confusion. None the less it should not be dismissed out of hand. If the burden of the accumulating indebtedness required for maintaining stability were of great dimensions, it should be taken seriously. But it is premature to make any such supposition, and the manifest inconveniences of the interest-free proposal are sufficient to rule it out for the time being. The government could meet a deficiency by borrowing at an average rate of about £80 millions a year and only increase the National Debt at the rate of one per cent. per annum. But if it issued paper money at the rate of £80 millions a year, the volume of money outstanding would be doubled in about five years. What confusion must result! It may be true that a deficiency of a given amount is no more inflationary if financed by an issue of paper money than if financed by borrowing, and that most of the additional issue of paper would be returned to the banks. But what of the banks? If their cash basis was increased at this unprecedented rate, they would have to revolutionize their normal practice. On what lines should they proceed? Would they continue to make a profit? They might be taken over by the state. It *may* happen that there will be other good reasons for taking them over in coming years. But it does not seem sensible to precipitate such a revolution merely in order to save the state a few millions of interest charge, a small fraction of what it is carrying with equanimity out of revenue for re-armament purposes (1936).

It remains to say something about the discouragement of saving. Taxation is a weapon. High rates of progression have probably already exerted a powerful force upon the very rich in this direction. Our chief danger in future may come from the middle classes and the undistributed profits of joint stock companies. Many expedients might be devised. I will only mention one. Insurance is coming to play a progressively more important part in our economic life. It is closely bound up with the activity of saving. I think of life insurance, pension funds, &c. Means might be found for extending insurance so as to cover a large part of the needs of the less well-to-do members of the community, whose aggregate savings are likely to be of increasing importance. My proposal would involve the nationalization of insurance.[1] It is a pre-eminently suitable business for public operation, since its activities are governed by mathematics and routine rather than by risk-taking and judgement.

The net saving involved by insurance is represented by the excess of premiums over disbursements. Vast funds are built up to cover liabilities. This building up is indispensable if insurance is to be operated by private enterprise. But in principle it is unnecessary. It is sufficient that the assets should cover any probable excess of disbursements over receipts. The principle is analogous to that by which a bank only holds a small proportion of its deposit liabilities in cash; but it has other assets. In the case of a nationalized insurance the other assets would be the general resources of the government. The excess of premiums over disbursements, which include accumulated interest, could be remitted to the Currency Equalization Account, which could proceed to plough it into the national revenue or build up a fighting fund to combat depressions. The total assets of British Insurance Companies show an increase between 1923 and 1933 of about £58 millions per annum, a considerable sum. The government would by this plan saddle itself with an immense potential uncovered liability. But this would never become an actual drain unless the people of the country suddenly abandoned the insurance habit.

The prospective needs of children are one cause of saving among the less well-to-do. A scheme for insurance against children—preferably compulsory and payable by bachelors also, with premiums in proportion to assessed income—might serve the double object of reducing the

[1] Or possibly only of insurance of the life insurance type.

untoward tendency towards over-saving and the calamitous decline of the birth-rate.

It must be observed once more, in conclusion, that these more radical proposals are only relevant if there is in fact a secular tendency on the part of a wealthy community to save too much. Whether this is so or not will probably only be known after remedies designed to avert cyclical depression have been put into operation.

IV. *Subsidies*

Additional measures of protection should not, in my judgement, be listed as a remedy available for regular use to combat depressions. This is not to deny that they are capable of being so used. The pure doctrine of Free Trade, as I understand it, does deny this. The extreme free trader holds that protection is not even a short-period palliative; the most he is prepared to admit is that it can be used to benefit a particular industry at the expense of certain others; but he holds that it cannot increase aggregate activity since what the protected industries gain in orders the exporting industries must lose. To this doctrine I should once have been prepared to subscribe. But the analysis of the dynamic determinants here set forth (see Chapter III, Section III) is inconsistent with it.[1] The following are the two most important arguments against the use of protective measures, one quasi-political and the other purely economic.

1. The first argument is that additional measures are unneighbourly, and unneighbourly conduct should be especially eschewed at a time of depression when all the world is suffering. Moreover it may provoke retaliation, which is capable of fully counteracting any stimulating effect that our own measures may have. Again, retaliation apart, we may suffer indirectly from our unneighbourliness,

---

[1] For a fuller discussion see also R. F. Harrod, *International Economics*, ch. ix, sec. 4.

for anything which aggravates depression abroad thereby adds to our difficulties by weakening our foreign markets. And the matter may be considered still more broadly. It is of vital importance to us on grounds other than economic that depression should not become too severe. For other nations seem apt to go slightly crazy under the scourge, and their craziness is bound to give us trouble in the long run. Illustration is unnecessary and might be invidious.

2. The second argument to which I refer is the basic principle of free trade, namely, that protection causes an uneconomic distribution of productive resources. This principle, propounded by Adam Smith, is the greatest definitive contribution of systematic economic thought, and it should always be borne in mind in economic planning. None the less I should not regard it as constituting by itself a final objection. The economists who stressed its importance in the last century had not in the forefront of their minds the problem of periodic under-employment. This is an evil which may reasonably be held to take priority over that of an uneconomic distribution of employment. Unfortunately it is improbable that any doctrine which an economist may offer regarding unemployment can be put forward with the same assurance of its correctness that may properly be attached to the free trade doctrine. But wise judgement may give priority to a doctrine, which only has probability on its side, about a more urgent problem, over an absolutely certain doctrine which relates to a less urgent one. This profession of weak allegiance to what may be called the basic principle of economics is not intended to suggest that, after all, protective measures may be regarded as a suitable remedy for the depression. For in that respect the first argument against protection appears to me decisive. The expression of weak allegiance is in place because the argument based upon the fundamental principle might be adduced against other remedial measures proposed. It does not hold

against banking policy or against a deficiency on current account, but it does hold, I fear, against unremunerative public works.

A reader might naturally entertain the notion that the proposals so far advanced are unduly roundabout and devious. Why not adopt a more direct and outright method of stimulating activity? Why not whip up the industries directly instead of approaching them through the channel of demand? I am not out of sympathy with this proposal, but it must be admitted that it is beset with serious difficulties.

When attention is directed to tinkering with particular industries, it is all too easy to forget that there is a general problem. The level of activity in the country is determined by the volume of current net investment and the multiplier, and the reorganization of an industry, if it affects neither of these, will merely make that industry expand at the expense of some other. Compulsory reorganization may be directed to making an industry more efficient in production or in its marketing methods. These improvements may be good in themselves, but will not touch the problem of under-employment. An exception must be registered in favour of improvements which make an increase of exports possible, since exports are a factor in one of the dynamic determinants (cf. Chapter III, Section III). Reorganization will also be beneficial if it increases net investment, as when an industry is prevented from raising fresh capital through being financially waterlogged and some compulsory pooling of interests is carried out. All these matters are worth looking into. Remedies of this kind, however, are not likely to be capable of rapid application and are therefore not of great importance for trade cycle purposes. Is it not possible, it may be asked, to find some remedy of general application that may be used to stimulate industries directly?

Unemployment is the greatest evil of depression. Is it not possible to attack this problem quite simply by offering a subsidy in respect of additional employment? The late Lord Melchett had a plan of this kind.[1]

An argument of fundamental economic interest in favour of the scheme may be noticed. When men are employed, their product is of a certain value to the community. If their remuneration does not exceed this value, private enterprise is likely to employ them and not otherwise. There is a consilience, it is held, between the interest of the community and that of their employer. For what is paid to the workers the community has to sacrifice out of its pool of available goods, and what the workers produce is thrown into that pool. If the value of the former falls short of that of the latter the community gains something by their employment and not otherwise. This contention, however, is not quite accurate. For if the workers are not employed, the community none the less parts with something to them; they do not starve and die, but receive unemployment insurance or assistance money or poor law relief and/or the private charity of friends and relations. What the community loses, therefore, by their being at work, is not the remuneration they receive, but that less the goods which they would somehow manage to consume, if out of work. If the value of their produce exceeds this loss to the community so computed, the community gains by their employment. But not so the private employer. He only gains if the value of their product is in excess of their wages. Consequently in order to get all the men employed, whose employment is of advantage to the community, the employer should receive a subsidy in respect of those whom he employs at the margin equal to the value of the goods which they would consume if out of work. This point, it may be noticed, is also relevant in computing the 'remunerativeness' of public works.

An objection to the scheme is the great administrative problems which it would involve. To subsidize all employment would be impracticable on the ground of

[1] Cf. Sir Alfred Mond, *The Remedy for Unemployment*, 1925.

expense; the proposal is to offer a subsidy to every firm in respect of each man employed during the year in excess of a certain basic number, thus confining the stimulus to the region in the neighbourhood of the margin. This might lead to the pooling of interests by firms, one firm transferring its orders to another, so that the latter would be able to draw a large subsidy, although the two together employed no more men than the basic number. The reader may imagine further complications. The administrative problem might not be insuperable, but it would be extremely complex.

It is necessary to examine the scheme in the light of our analysis. A distinction must be drawn between industries making capital goods and those making consumable goods. First suppose the subsidy confined to the former. Its effect would be to reduce the relative prices of capital goods. Since the volume of orders for capital goods depends on the relation between their cost and their prospective yield, the relative fall in their price should be a stimulus to net investment and so, via the multiplier, to activity generally. The scheme would produce a result analogous to a low rate of interest in stimulating net investment. It is deserving of serious consideration.

What would be the effect of dispensing the subsidy more widely to the whole of industry? This generalization of the subsidy would, it appears, remove the special stimulus to net investment, for there would be no *relative* fall in the prices of capital goods, consequent upon it. Would it stimulate activity generally?

The answer to this question appears to depend upon how the subsidy was raised. We are faced with the difficulty that unless net investment is stimulated the general level of income cannot move upwards because of the multiplier. If the subsidy was financed by loans there is no doubt that it would be stimulating. But in this case the subsidy method falls into the general class of expedients which involve the piling up of public indebtedness.

Moreover, if the subsidy is raised in this way, there is no need to go through the ritual of making it in respect of additional men employed, with all the administrative difficulties which that involves. *Any* series of subsidies, raised by loan, and distributed among industries equitably or inequitably, would have a similar effect in stimulating activity.

What if the subsidy were raised by taxation?[1] Then it appears that the effectiveness of the subsidy would depend on whether or not it stimulated the capital goods industries; if there is no stimulus there it would seem that general activity cannot rise. Whether a generalized subsidy would stimulate the capital goods industries is a problem the analysis of which is extremely difficult without the introduction of a dangerously large number of assumptions. But one conclusion leaps to the eye. The effectiveness of the stimulus depends precisely on how much the production of capital goods is stimulated. The effect of a given subsidy is more likely to be large if confined to the capital goods industries, since it would alter the relative prices of capital and consumable goods. Therefore, if the subsidy is to be raised by taxation, it would be wise to confine it to the capital goods industries.

Our conclusions so far are as follows:

1. If the subsidies are raised by loans, they, like other increases of public indebtedness, have a stimulating effect. In this case there is no need to incur the administrative trouble of making the subsidy conditional on the number of men employed by the firms receiving it. The expedient is worth considering because it may be that loans raised for the purpose of giving direct help to industries might encounter less opposition from public opinion than loans raised to finance a budgetary deficiency.

2. If the subsidies are raised by taxation they should

[1] This might have some of the stimulating effect of a subsidy raised by loan if it decreased the propensity to save.

be confined to capital goods industries. In this case, unfortunately, the ritual of making the subsidy depend on the number of men employed or some similar criterion[1] would be necessary. A subsidy raised by taxation that does not operate in such a way as to give an inducement to produce more than would be produced in its absence will have no stimulating effect on general activity. The disadvantage entailed by the complex administrative problems involved might be thought to point away from this expedient to subsidies raised by loan. But against this disadvantage may be set the great advantage that we have at last found a form of stimulus which does not involve the piling up of public indebtedness.

One further possibility remains to be considered. It has been assumed that general activity cannot be stimulated by any method that does not alter the value of net investment or of the multiplier. But, strictly, in place of general activity should be written the general level of income. Is it possible that some method of subsidy, possibly combined with a system of penalties, could be devised, which would raise the level of activity without raising the level of income, or, better, without raising the amount which people would choose at their new level of income to save? It must be remembered that prime factors of production are not such large savers as profit-takers. Suppose, for the sake of argument, that the prime factors save nothing. Could a system of penalties and bonuses be imposed in such a way as to make it worth the entrepreneurs' while to produce more, and at the same time leave them with no more profit than they would have received in the absence of the scheme? If we suppose, as we must, that the prime factors do save something, albeit not on a large scale, it

[1] It is possible that the amount of output, if this could be measured quantitatively, would be a better criterion than the amount of employment, because this would prevent the subsidy from stimulating the use of uneconomic methods of production, viz. those using too much labour, which besides being uneconomic would have the disadvantage that they might have an adverse effect on net investment.

would be necessary for the system to leave the profit-takers with rather less profit than they would have in its absence.

Reference was made to penalties. In order to secure the required inducement to maintain output it might be necessary to penalize by progressive fines the firms which allowed their output to relapse. Indeed, in this way the scheme might be made self-supporting like the pool of a cartel, the fines imposed on some being used to pay the bounties meted out to others. The reference to a cartel is timely; those who fear that a scheme of fines and bounties is too complex to be practical may be reminded that such schemes have actually been worked by numerous cartels. But there is a fundamental difference between the cartel devices and ours. For the former are used to encourage restriction while ours is designed to encourage expansion.

The arguments of this section suggest that subsidies are worthy of investigation as a method of averting a recession. In their case, as in that of other remedies, quick action and, therefore, preparation of the ground are essential.

The earlier chapters of this essay claim to present a precise diagnosis of the causes of the trade cycle. The present chapter cannot be said to do more than present matter for reflection.

INDEX

81

83
85
82